PALMISTRY
THE MYSTERY OF DESTINY

SUNITA CHABRA

ISBN 978-93-81115-72-5
© Sunita Chabra, 2011

Cover Design   Mishta Roy
Layouts   Ajay Shah, Mumbai
Printing   Repro India Ltd, Navi Mumbai

Published in India 2011 by
CELESTIAL BOOKS
An imprint of
LEADSTART PUBLISHING PVT LTD
Trade Centre, Level 1, Bandra Kurla Complex
Bandra (E), Mumbai 400 051, INDIA
T + 91 22 40700804   F +91 22 40700800
E info@leadstartcorp.com   W www.leadstartcorp.com

US Office
Axis Corp
7845 E Oakbrook Circle
Madison, WI 53717, USA

All rights reserved worldwide
No part of this publication may be reproduced, stored in or introduced into a retrieval system, or transmitted, in any form, or by any means (electorinic, mechanical, photocopying, recording or otherwise), without the prior permission of the Publisher. Any person who commits an unauthorised act in relation to this publication can be liable to criminal prosecution and civil claims for damages.

Disclaimer The views expressed in this book are those of the Author and do not pertain to be those held by the Publisher.

In Gratitude

I thank God, who dwells in my heart. You poured thoughts into my mind in the sweetest of ways, and I wrote all of them down in this book.

I thank my family for all the support they have provided me over the years.

My immense gratitude to my publisher, but most of all, to my readers.

ABOUT THE AUTHOR

SUNITA CHABRA is an internationally acclaimed, professional astrologer, numerologist and palmist. A Chemistry graduate from Delhi University, Sunita did her Masters in Social Statistics from the University of Southampton, UK. She has also been awarded the titles of *Jyotish Prabhakar* and *Jyotish Shastri* (equivalent to Bachelors and Masters degrees in Vedic Astrology).

Sunita has been a practicing consultant for over 12 years and is a member of the Research Group for the Critical Study of Astrology, UK.

She has contributed numerous articles and forecast columns to leading newspapers and magazines including the *Times of India*, *Savvy*, *New Woman* and *Indian-American Newspaper*. Her work has also found mention in the *Washington Post*. Many of Sunita's accurate predictions can be retrieved and verified from newspaper archives.

Sunita has also taught Vedic astrology at the Online American College of Astrology and been featured extensively on both television and radio. Her first book, *Zodiac Guide 2009*, was published in 2008. Sunita can be contacted at: **sunita_chabra@yahoo.com**

CONTENTS

Foreword   6

PART I
1. Right Hand or Left Hand?   9
2. The Thumb   16
3. Introduction to the Hand   34
4. Meaning of Lines on the Palm   47
5. Love, Marriage & Relationships   63
6. Money & Career   78
7. Travel   105
8. Children   110
9. Spirituality   117
10. Illness & Disease   122

PART II Destiny Paths of the Rich & Famous   132
Hand of Barrack Obama, President, USA   133
Hand of Vladimir Putin, Prime Minister, Russia   138
Handprint of Albert Einstein, Scientist   142
Hand of Sonia Gandhi, Leader, Congress Party   146
Hand Cast of Michael Jackson, Musician   150
Hand of Charles, Prince of Wales   154
Hand of Nicole Kidman, Actress   158
Hand of Benazir Bhutto, Politician   161
Hand of Hillary Clinton, Secretary of State, USA   164

FOREWORD

karmanyevaadhikaaraste maa phaleshu kadaachana |
maa karmaphalaheturbhuu maatesangotsvakarmani ||
Your right is to work only, never to the fruits thereof
Never be motivated by the fruits of the action,
nor be attached to inaction
~ *Bhagavad Gita* [2: 47]

MANY HISTORIANS BELIEVE that the science of palmistry originated in India. In my professional experience as an astrologer and palmist, I have found Hindu palmistry amazingly mystifying – having studied many published and some unpublished, ancient works on Hindu palmistry and then verified them in my professional practise. The works of ancient Western palmists are as valuable, but the hidden secrets and gems of Hindu palmistry have not been fully explored.

And now, after years of my own professional work of mapping the past, present and future, I feel it is time to share that knowledge and experience. This book contains fresh and original material drawn from that personal experience and knowledge. An inquisitive and scientific bent of mind and an educational background in science, helped me in my endeavour to understand palmistry. It is my belief that the present volume is the most extensive work that has ever been published, combining ancient Hindu and Western palmistry.

Palmistry is the cryptic code of life. A soul takes birth with his/her destiny code and manual written on the hands. The brain stores the information about all our past births as also the blueprint for our present life. According to science, the nerves carry currents and messages from the brain to the hands, and palmists believe these same nerves carry the destiny cryptic code from our brain to our hands, even though we do not remember our past births or our present destiny plan – probably because of *karmic* amnesia.

Before we reject this theory, let us verify for ourselves its validity and study palmistry first. Perhaps carry out statistical research on any one palm line and its inference on a group. No knowledge that has a long history, like palmistry does, should be rejected before carrying out scientific research in close association with an informed palmist. Learn about it, research it, test it, evaluate it, and then see if it is accurate.

I have added a special chapter on spirituality, based on what life has taught me and what I am still learning, as also from my experiences as a palmist in reading and understanding from the lives of others. Though, I have an educational background in science, my reading of ancient Hindu scriptures and my experience as a palmist, changed my perspective on life. I do not in any way, wish to impose my beliefs on my readers – I merely share them with my readers. Among the misery and sorrows of the present world, I write with the hope in my heart that this knowledge may help people in some way. The chapter on spirituality has been added to help us understand the bigger picture of life and move in the direction of peace and happiness in *this* journey of life.

The spiritual path is not necessarily related to religion, so people of all faiths can follow it. Knowledge of palmistry and knowing something of the future but not using that knowledge to make improvements, is but a waste. If we understand there is bigger picture of life, beyond what we eat or wear, it may help us become more complete human beings. The spiritual path makes us more aware of our actions – *karma*. We are all human and the journey of life is not easy. Learn to avoid the potholes. Palmistry can also work like psycho-therapy in times of crisis.

So let us begin our study to decode the mysterious Map of Destiny imprinted on our hands, called Palmistry.

Part I: 1
RIGHT HAND OR LEFT HAND?

MANY BOOKS HAVE been published on the subject of palmistry – how this book is different from the others can only be decided by my readers. In these pages, I have combined my own professional experience and educational background in science, with the knowledge handed down by ancient Hindu and Western palmists.

Palmistry is the 'study of the hand' and the various signs on it. Lines that run across the palm, the mounts (or fleshy parts) of the palm, and the structure of the fingers, hold the secret to your past and future. Everything that you were born with when you came into this world, who you are today, and what you will be in future, is indicated on your hands. It is like a code that you need to decipher. It is not fatalistic – it is not just your past, but present *karma* as well that determines your destiny. The Almighty has probably placed this code of destiny in your hands to emphasize the power of your present *karma*.

The human mind has conscious and sub-conscious parts – perhaps the imprints on the palm are caused by the workings of the sub-conscious mind which is a store-house of all our *karma* from many previous births. In palmistry, curiously, each feature and line of the hand has its own meaning and foretells the events of one's life. Smaller lines change (present *karma*), but the major lines (past *karma*), remain unchanged.

Right Hand or Left Hand?
According to science, the brain in human beings, is the centre of the nervous system. The brain receives signals from sensory nerves in the body. There are nerves running from the brain to our hands.

It is also believed by many, that the brain stores the broad map of our destiny. Why are we not consciously aware of this? Scientific research suggests, on an average, a human being uses only 10% of his brain in his entire life. What it suggests is that we may be consciously aware of only 10% of our brain activity, but it does not mean that the other 90% is not working, only that we are not consciously aware of its activity. On a situational level, it is clear we do repetitive tasks in our daily life, without consciously being aware of it.

What I am suggesting, and which all scientists may not agree with, but cannot give scientific proofs to disagree with either, is the 'unused' 90% of the brain is capable of storing our inherited *karmas* (of past lives) or the memory of past lives, though we may not be consciously be aware of it! Clearly, the brain is a vastly complex organ with a myriad possibilities. The mystical inner world of human beings is in fact, far greater and far clearer than our usual sense of reality. Science has not got all the answers to all the 'whys'. Science may slowly, in the future, unravel the various integrative factors involved in this mystery.

Now the primary question to ask is: which hand to read – the right or left? The second question is: are the same rules for reading the hands applicable for both men and women? There is so much confusion about this matter!

Let us address the first question – which hand to read? It has been established in medical sciences that the left side of the brain interacts with the right side of the body, and the right side of the brain interacts with the left side of the body. The reason for this cross-connection of the brain with the body is still not clear. According to medical science, the verbal, sorting, detail-oriented side of the brain is on the left, whereas the spatial, intuitive, nonverbal side is placed on the right. Following the logic of science and applying the mystique of palmistry, this implies that the right side of the brain is the intuitive and less consciously aware side and stores the broad map of our destiny and our past *karma*, whereas the left side of the brain is our present *karma* and our will.

As there is a cross-connection of the brain with the body, the left hand is what we are born with and the right hand is what we make of our life. This is true for right handed people and vice-a-versa for left-handed people. The fruits of our past *karma*, along with our destiny plan, is written on our left hand. How we mix our destiny plan with present *karma*, depends on our intelligence and will power. If we are strong both intellectually and spiritually, we will be able to overcome road blocks laid in our destiny plan but if we are weak as human beings, fear, greed, emotions or for other reasons, we may even spoil the promised fruits. All this can be read on the right hand. Our personality and circumstances bring changes in our life. So read the left hand to know what you are born with and the right hand to know how changes affect your life.

The second question is whether the same rules for reading hands applied to both men and women? In ancient Hindu palmistry, the left hand for women and the right hand for men, is suggested. This implies that for men, the left hand gives the destiny plan they are born with (linked with the intuitive or passive part of the brain), and the right hand (linked with the active part of the brain), is what they make of their lives. It is vice-a-versa for women.

Now the question to ask is: are there really large differences between the male and female brain? Scientific research suggests, yes, there are. I am including only two of the many scientific researches in the subject, for lack of space and to keeping the focus on the main purpose of writing this book – to underpin palmistry with scientific logic. The multiplicity of similarities and differences between male and female brains is given at glance in Table 1 [Source: Dr. Marian C. Diamond, Prof. of Anatomy/Neuro-Anatomy, University of California, Berkeley, USA].

If we combine ancient Hindu palmistry knowledge with scientific research, reading the left hand for women and the right hand for men, **as active hands, seems correct.** Biologically, men and women are programmed differently, so it seems logical to follow Hindu palmistry norms of reading different hands for men and women.

Of course, **for the complete reading of past, present and future**, both the right and the left hands should be closely examined. We all want the best for ourselves, but not all of us get what we want in life. Variations in the lines of both hands would suggest changes in personality and circumstances. Changes in life are inevitable, whether we want them or not. What destiny has for you and what efforts you are making to achieve the same, for this, both hands should be read. I personally look at both hands, for what changes a person is trying to bring and whether his efforts will bring fruitful results or not.

Palmistry also lays importance on our present *karma* or actions. God has given us the power to bring about some changes in our destiny that we can only do through our *karma*. Enlightenment of the soul is very important. Unless we understand the importance of our actions and thoughts, we cannot bring improvements into our lives and find happiness on this earth. Evil, in the form of war, greed, lust and jealousy, can only bring disease and unhappiness. Each of us, through our individual efforts (*karmas*), can bring peace, happiness and tranquility to our individual lives and eventually this collective effort of individuals, can bring peace and happiness to our planet. Changes at the atomic level can bring structural changes.

Palmistry highlights how destiny is in our hands, and if we want love, money and happiness (which all human beings want), we only have to make improvements in our *karma*. We have to learn to select our thoughts and discard all negative thoughts when they surface in our heads. By keeping only positive thoughts in our heads, we can bring about radical changes to our lives. The past cannot be changed but the future is in our hands.

You should understand here that the objective of my including scientific research throughout this book is to add a different perspective to palmistry, beyond predictions. In the present, uncertain and difficult times, rife with war, economic recession and disease, palmistry on a broader level teaches us to enlighten our souls and be good human beings.

On the active hand, you yourself will see changes in the lines, and improvements in your life. These may be slow but they are definite changes. Imagine how such an understanding can bring changes to our society and to mankind on this earth.

Science is so powerful in present times that any stream of thought, be it astrology, *ayurveda*, homeopathy, yoga, etc, obtains recognition only if science validates it. Otherwise, it continues to bear the tag of 'superstition', or in the language of science, is a 'placebo effect'. Beliefs find approval not on their own merits, but within the methodology and parameters set by greater science. It would seem that beliefs and science are two sides of a sphere, when one is light the other remains in darkness!

TABLE I

Age (days)		N	Cortical Areas						
			Frontal	Parietal			Occipital		
			10	4	3	2	18	17	18A
Males	6	13	S	S	S	NS	S	S	S
	14	17	S	S	S	NS	S	S	S
	20	15	S	S	S	NS	S	S	NS
	90	15	NS	S	S	NS	NS	S	NS
	185	15	S	NS	S	S	S	S	S
	400	15	S	NS	S	S	S	S	NS
	900	8	NS	NS	NS	NS	NS	NS	NS
All Ss R>L									
Females	7	15	NS	NS	NS	NS	NS	NS	NS
	14	15	NS	NS	NS	NS	NS	NS	NS
	21	15	NS	NS	S#	NS	NS	NS	NS
	90	19	NS	NS	NS	NS	NS	NS	NS
	180	11	NS	NS	NS	NS	NS	NS	NS
	390	17	NS	NS	S#	NS	NS	NS	NS

S#=L>R

Sources [S = statistically significant; NS = non-statistically significant]
* Statistical significance of differences between right and left cerebral cortical thickness in male and female rats: Dr. Marian Diamond, Prof. of Anatomy/Neuro-Anatomy, University of California, Berkeley
* *On average, male and female minds are of a slightly different character and this distinction arises from biology not culture.* Simon Baron-Cohen, Director, Autism Research Centre, Cambridge University

Part I:II
THE THUMB
Past *Karma* + Personality/Character + Present *Karma*
= Our DESTINY/FATE

THIS BOOK MAY help my readers to decipher their own destiny/fate from their hands. The personality or character of a person mixes with the 'past' and this decides how things will happen 'now'. Actions or decisions taken now, in the present, will decide what may happen 'tomorrow', in the future. What may happen tomorrow, however, also has a certain part over which we have no control at all.

There are two kinds of events in life – those over which we have control and those over which we have no control (for instance, who our parents are). The personality or a character of a person can only influence the part which, as mortal human beings, we have control over. The part we have no control over, is guided by our past lives and *karma*.

The personality or character of a person. to a very great extent, influences destiny. After all, what we do (*our karma*), necessarily depends on what kind of human beings we are. The character of a person and its influence over his/her destiny plan, can be read from the thumb. I have been practicing principles of *Nadi* astrology with palmistry in my professional readings. *Nadi* astrology is a form of astrology practiced in India in which the thumb and the markings on the thumb are really very important.

Those who have a long thumb and a long line head, especially starting from the mount of power, the mount of Jupiter; attain position and power in their lifetime. In Part II, *The Destiny Paths Of The Rich And Famous,* you can read more about the importance of long thumbs in the destiny of powerful people.

The thumb, in palmistry, is considered to be the centre of will-power and logical thinking in a person. The thumb is largely considered to be divided into two parts or phalanges – the first, or the phalange containing the nail, indicates will-power, and the second phalange indicates logical thinking. If the first phalange is longer than the second phalange, then it can be interpreted to mean that the person has strong will power and can face challenges in life. If the second phalange is longer than the first or waist like thumb, it can be interpreted to mean that the person has good reasoning powers and takes logical decisions but may lack the will power to execute them. If both the phalanges are of the same size, it means the person has a good balance of will power and reason.

Different Types of Thumbs and their Lengths

The length of the thumb can be estimated, if you place it close to the first finger of the hand. The thumb is said to be of normal length if the tip of the thumb reaches till about the base of the forefinger. If it reaches above the base of the forefinger, then it is said to be of long length; and if below the base of the forefinger, then the thumb is said to be of short length. The higher the tip of the thumb reaches on the first finger of the hand (when the thumb is held close to the other fingers), the stronger and more powerful the person will be. The length of the thumb indicates the average development of the brain.

Several research studies have shown that the colour, length and breadth of the thumb depends on country, race and gender. People of some countries or races may generally be tall, so while making predictions, this factor should be taken into account.

Long Thumb

Those who have long thumbs, possess strong will power, high intellect and are self-dependent. Generally, presidents, prime ministers, heads of the state, and others who hold important position in life, have long thumbs. The larger the **thumb**, the greater are the chances of success in life.

Short Thumb

Those who have short thumbs, give more importance to emotions than logical thinking and are often dependent on others to take decisions for them. They may take special interest in poetry, painting or music.

Medium Thumb
Those who have a medium length of thumb, have a balance between will power and logical thinking. Generally, average success (professional and monetary), can be predicted for a person with such a thumb.

Flexibility of the Thumb
The flexibility of the thumb is the measure of your flexibility in life. The ability of a person to adapt, change or make adjustments in life is very important and a big learning experience for the soul. In life, we do not necessarily get what we desire. The kind of people we meet and the situations we go through, are also not in our hands. One of the biggest challenges of life is to learn to make compromises, whether in work, relationships, marriage and even with oneself. Yes, even with oneself. Why? Because we all have dreams, ambitions, hopes and desires, but we do have limitations and shortcomings too, that we somehow do not want to see or understand. Unless we understand ourselves, we cannot be good human beings. Our limitations and shortcomings bring fear, jealousy, frustration, depression, anger, failures and eventually all this leads to unhappiness, depression, illness and disease.

I believe that the most important aim or goal in life should be happiness and contentment. That is not to say we should not be ambitious, but we should be happy and contended people first. When we are happy and contended within, we make the earth a better place to live in. Each and every particle around us gets charged with positive energy and this energy is transmitted to other human beings. What good are palaces, money and position if we are not happy?

Check the flexibility of your thumb, and make corrections in your own personality. Do not be ashamed to admit your flaws – we all have them and it takes a lot of courage to admit it. The thumb can be:
- stiff
- slightly bending/supple
- soft

Stiff Thumb
A stiff thumb stands erect and does not bend easily. No amount of pressure will bend this thumb farther back. Such a person is practical, economical and stubborn in temperament. He/she will stick to their judgment or point of view, and the more he/she is opposed, the more determined he/she will be to hold on. However, such people are stable in love and relationships. Those who have stiff thumbs, would like to have stable homes and single stable partners. Fidelity is an important issue with them and they are monogamous by nature. It is a different thing that the partner may have to make many adjustments to maintain a happy home.

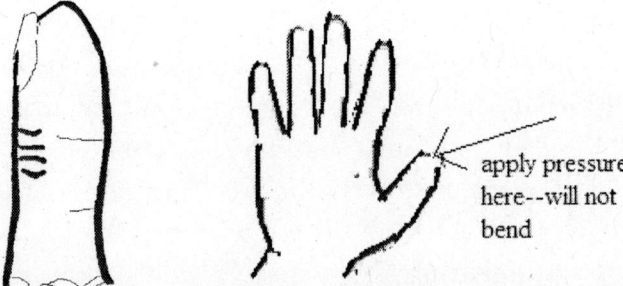

Figure 1: The Stiff Thumb

The pillar-shaped thumb at the tip does not bend backwards but is straight and erect. Such a person, though he himself may not be so, attracts a lot of cynicism, negativity and enmity. Relationships are difficult for such a person. People with such a thumb should learn to bend. To attract tranquility and harmony in life, such people need to make a few changes to their personality. The quicker they learn, the more peaceful life becomes. What could be more valuable in life than one's own peace of mind and happiness? When we make adjustments to our personality, it is not as if we are doing it for someone else – we are doing it for ourselves.

Slightly Bending/Supple Thumb

Figure 2: The Supple Thumb

The shape of this thumb is like a sword. A supple thumb bends slightly and beautifully. This denotes a balanced nature and someone who is pliable and adaptable to others. A person with such a thumb is generally successful in life. This could be because he/she is more adaptable to changing times and is not obstinate in his/her views. Such a person makes fewer enemies, who may otherwise erect blocks in the road to success. Developmental outcomes in life are influenced by temperament in an individual. The thumb reflects overall development of mind and body. Several statistical studies also show that persons with strong will power and good adaptability in relationships, are the most likely to benefit in life.

Soft Thumb

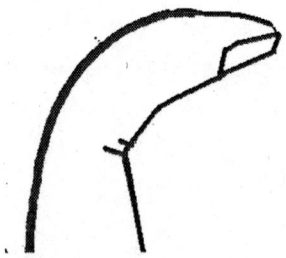

Figure 3: The Soft Thumb

The supple thumb bends outwards like an arrow. Generally, such persons are clear hearted. For personal peace and tranquility, they bend and accept what life has to offer. In my experience, I have seen people with such thumbs are generally married to a very strong headed spouse and/or at work, the boss or business partner is stubborn and quick tempered. To avoid friction, they bend and accept things as they are. However, in their own lives, this brings mental strain and little happiness. Whenever dark cloud of uncertainty and difficulty loom over such a person, he/she tries to find ways to escape.

If possible, he/she should make an effort to control his/her emotions with the desire to succeed. This is how present *karma* will win over past *karmas*. You may not be programmed to behave in a certain way, but knowledge of palmistry can help you. Rather than being an escapist, stand firm and face the fear. Success always hides behind fear, uncertainties and setbacks.

If the tip or the face of the thumb is not broad, such a person may even suffer from weakness of nerves or anxiety. It is sad but true that an unhappy person is unable to attract success. Research studies indicate inner peace and satisfaction brings success, improved relationships and better health. The day-to-day life of a happy person moves more smoothly. I am mentioning this here to help people with such a thumb to develop a bright and happy outlook towards life. The face of the thumb is an indication of the will power of the person in facing challenges. Our thoughts and will power have great control over our lives. If we often think about difficulties and miseries in life, then that is what we get, and if we tend to think about success, we do attract success.

There is no major law of science or amazing miraculous phenomenon operating here, but simply that this indicates the programming of our minds and the relationship to happiness. When a person transforms the energy of desire and positive insight into action, he/she begins the walk towards success and happiness.

Palmistry and astrology go together and that is what I have been practicing professionally for many years. Ancient books of the *Nadi* systems (astro-palmistry), have delineated how to prepare horoscopes from palm prints. Ancient Hindu palmistry gives a better approach towards the predictive part of palmistry, but I will also include a few signs given in Runic and Egyptian palmistry. I am giving only those signs on the thumb that I have used in my professional experience, and which have given amazingly accurate predictions. I am listing them below (figure 4) and including the lines found on the thumb. The signs that I have listed are rare and not commonly found. However, the lines on the thumb are not rare but are very important in predictions and have special meanings.

Signs on the Thumb in Hindu Palmistry

These signs, found anywhere on thumb, have the same meaning.

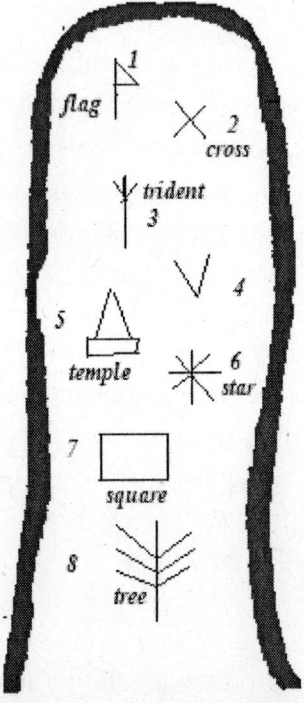

Figure 4: Hindu palmistry signs on the thumb

1. **Flag sign**: this sign, when found on the face of the thumb, indicates that the person will be famous and will enjoy high social status. Politicians and people in prominent positions may have this sign. When found touching any main line on the thumb (next section), it enhances the meaning of that line.

2. **Cross/ plus sign**: if this sign is found on the face of the thumb, in astro-palmistry this means Saturn, *Rahu-ketu* (nodes of moon) or planet Mars is placed in the ascendant or preceding/succeeding house to ascendant. When this sign becomes dark, the person having this sign may incur losses, expenditures, health problems or obstacles in life.

3. **Trident/ *trishul***: the trident/*trishul* is a Hindu religious symbol associated with Hindu deities. It is considered to be an auspicious sign in palmistry. The three prongs of the trident/*trishul* signify prosperity, spirituality and abundance. This sign, when found anywhere on the thumb, brings luck. It is believed that such a person carries positive accumulated actions from his/her previous births – *sanchit karmas*.

4. **V Mark or angle**: the V mark is also a Hindu religious symbol and is associated with Lord Vishnu, the Creator. This sign on a thumb brings respectability, social status and growth in life. However, such a person has to face a few ups and downs in life too. Hard times more than good times add dimension to one's personality. Life is a learning process. Failure and success are two sides of a coin and living life in

this contrast helps us value and appreciate life more. Can success and more success only, make us happy? When we taste failure or setbacks, we realize the importance of the other. What matters the most is how much we learn from these experiences and how, as human beings, we grow. The main aim of any soul is not just to acquire wealth or build houses, but for the soul to spiritually evolve during the journey on earth. The V sign on the thumb helps us evolve as better human beings.

5. **Star**: the star, found anywhere on the thumb, means something unexpected and sudden, but when found on the second phalange near the base of the thumb, it means a sudden, unexpected windfall, legacy, inheritance, lottery or enormous wealth.

6. **Square**: the square is a sign of preservation. It protects the person from money loss/bankruptcy, defamation, illness and other adversities. In some cases I have seen, it is found to bring improvements/gains in house and property.

7. **Tree**: this is an extraordinary sign when found on the thumb. In Hindu palmistry, this sign is called *Kalpa Vriksha*, the Sacred Tree. It fulfills all desires, hopes and ambitions in the lifetime of the person on whose hand it is found.

I am including three more signs as given in Runic palmistry, that I have used in my professional experience.

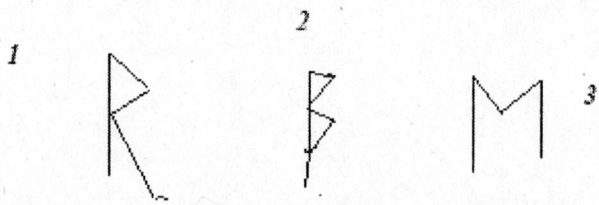

Figure 5: The Runic palmistry signs on the thumb

1. **Raidho**: this sign, when found on the second phalange of the thumb, denotes travel.

2. **Beorc**: if this sign touches the important main lines of the thumb (next section), it means new beginnings.

3. **Ehwaz**: when this sign when touches the important main lines of the thumb, it brings new beginnings or opens a new chapter of life. Sign 'm' probably stands for money or marriage.

Lines on the Thumb in Hindu Palmistry
Look at figure 6: if not all, you will find many of these lines on your own thumb. I have interpreted these lines slightly differently from traditional ancient palmistry and found them to be true in practice. This, I believe, should be done to take into account how times have changed.

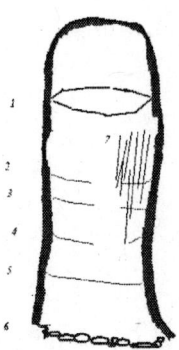

Figure 6: Hindu palmistry lines on the thumb

1. **Wheat line or *Pushpa Rekha*:** in Hindi, *Pushapa* means 'flower' and probably this line, as the name suggests, shows how a person will bloom in life. This line is found between the first and second phalanges of the thumb. The Wheat line or *Pushpa Rekha* may be in the shape of an eye, straight line or it could even be broken or dented. It is common to have more than one line or two parallel wheat lines.

    If the wheat line is in the shape of an eye, the possessor is lucky and never lacks in basic amenities like food etc, in life. If a straight line is found between the first two phalanges of the thumb, also if it is dented, the possessor has to struggle for day-to-day living. Surprisingly, I have found this line on the hands of those who have uncertainty over their income for instance, on the hands of daily wagers, or on the hands of those whom we employ as helping hands at home.

If you have one straight line and a line parallel to it – it means your expenditure will be high – that is, money will flow in and flow out. To know the timing of events, divide this line into three parts: the first part will be the first half of life; the second part will be one's middle age; and the third part will be the twilight or later years of life. If total life expectancy is presumed to be 80 years, then the centre of this line would mean ages 38-42 years. Calculation of age should start from the side where the fingers are and towards the side where thumb is joined with the wrist.

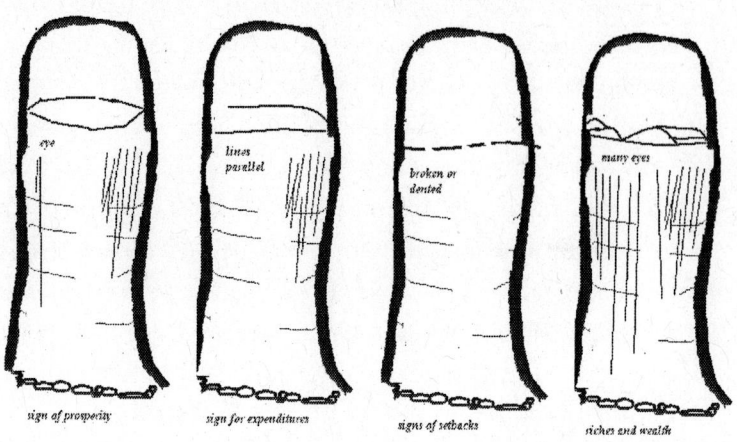

Figure 6.1: The Wheat lines on the thumb

2. *Madhura Rekha*: *rekha* means 'line' and *madhura* means 'sweet as nectar', in Hindi. This line indicates the sweetness of soul. Spiritual, humane, philanthropists and charitable persons, will have this line. Mostly this line is small and found only on the sides of the thumb. Of

course, a person has to experience life to evolve as a better human being. Some are born with a certain maturity, but most have to experience the ups and downs of life to acquire understanding. There are many who go through the journey of life without understanding the actual meaning of life. Pursuing career goals, land acquisition, money and relationships are important, but can they be the ultimate goals of our life? It is all *maya*, illusion, as per Hindu belief. In a dream we travel to different places, meet many known or unknown people, experience different emotions, but when we open our eyes, only then does the realization come that it was not real but only a dream. Life is very similar – only when we open our inner eye do we understand the true meaning of life. Whenever this line appears on the thumb, life from then on becomes sweet as nectar. We see everyday life with different eyes, and it has a fresh meaning. This change in perspective brings happiness and many positive developments.

3. *Mandara Rekha*: *rekha* means 'line' and *mandara* could refer to Mount Mandara, a mythical mountain mentioned in the *Puranas*, the ancient holy books of the Hindus. The mountain, in a mythological tale, was used by the gods as a stick to churn the ocean. This line reflects the possibilities of foreign travel (crossing of oceans to see far-away lands).

4. *Mana rekha*: *rekha* means 'line' and in Sanskrit, *mana* means 'mind'. Numerous thoughts go through our minds in a day. We all are constantly 'in' thought while awake. Here, mind refers to many wants and desires in

personal relationships. This line is found only when a person has a plurality of relationships.

5. **Rati Rekha**: in Hinduism, *Rati* is the goddess of passion and lust and *rekha* means 'line'. Western and other palmists, derive relationships from the fate line, the mounts of Venus, Jupiter and Mercury. But in Hindu palmistry, *Rati Rekha* indicates marriage, and also the kind of relationship the couple will share. When this line has a dot, is broken, dented, crossed or has an island (see Figure 6.2), this indicates problems in relationships. If there is a subsidiary line/s above or below this line, it means more than one marriage or relationship. If there is a black dot or scissor lines (bar), on this line, it indicates an unpleasant legal divorce. If this line is broken in many parts, there is an increased possibility of marriage not occurring at all.

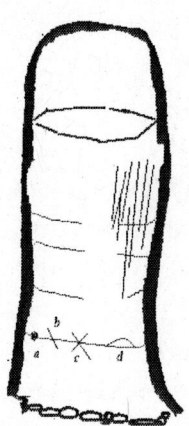

Figure 6.2: The signs on the line of marriage
a= dot; b=bar; c=cross; d=island

6. **Malika Rekha**: *rekha* means 'line' and *malika* comes from Sanskrit, meaning 'a white sweet smelling flower – Jasmine. This line, together with the Wheat Line (Line 1), in my experience, is very helpful in predicting past, present and future. This line is found at the base of the thumb where the thumb meets the palm. Where and when this line is broken, at that age there will be changes in life. A dot or cross indicates there may be loss of health. When this line is thin and long; there is the sign of an eye on wheat line; and the palm is pink rose in colour; the person will have great wealth and happy relations with his/her spouse and children. When there are auspicious signs (flag, triangle, fish, tree), the person will rise in social and economic status. Dents or the Z sign on this line means a period of great change in life. If there in a vertical line running from the centre of the *Malika Rekha* towards the face of the thumb, some legal problems or great problem caused by enmity, is possible.

7. **Kesar Rekha**: *Kesar* in Hindi means saffron and *rekha* means 'line'. Saffron is the colour associated with the planet Jupiter – the planet of growth, prosperity, happiness and good luck. These are vertical lines on the thumb. There will be more unhappiness and struggles in life if these vertical lines are missing on the thumb. I have found them to be amazingly accurate in my predictions. The age when these lines appear on the thumb (read line 1 for time estimation), there are opportunities for growth and happiness in life. If these line/s are thick, there will be obstacles and problems on the work-front and in one's personal life.

The difference in not having and having thick line/s is major. In the former case, when this line is completely missing, there may be no growth opportunity and resultant stagnancy, hence frustration. In the latter case, when this line is present but is thick, there will *be* opportunities but the path of success will be full of obstacles and problems. When this line is not missing in the first part of the thumb but is well marked in the second part, it means the person will have a difficult childhood – both emotionally and financially, but will enjoy a good career and relationships from the age when these lines appear – that is, change of circumstances bringing wealth and prosperity.

It is best to have thin and hair-like *kesar* lines for happiness and prosperity. However, if these lines are very faint, barely visible, and need a magnifying glass to see, in that case there will be growth, wealth and prosperity but one may also have to face weak health, jealousy, ego problems and discord in relationships. When this line proceeds in a serpentine fashion from line 6, that is from *Malika Rekha*, towards the phalanges, anxiety and nervous disorders in life are possible. General growth, prosperity and happiness in life are observed from these lines.

Part I: III
INTRODUCTION TO THE HAND
Shape of the Hand ~ Fingers ~ Mounts

THIS CHAPTER IS MORE of an introduction for those who are new to palmistry. I am outlining here, what each line, mount and finger means and their significance in predictive palmistry, to familiarize my readers with these basics. I have explained in separate chapters, how to read love, marriage, career, money or health from the hand. This book is not written to teach palmistry, but so my readers can read their own hands and steer their lives in the right direction. If you are going through a low phase of your life, read in your hand when this phase will change. After all, no phase whether good or bad, remains in life forever. It is about learning to be more positive during low phases and more humble during the good phases of life. Nothing remains same forever and this is an eternal truth.

In palmistry, one must remember that no one sign stands alone and the entire hand must be read in totality and interpreted in reference to each other for accurate predictions. Even the manner of opening the palm is significant and reveals the personality of the individual and his/her level of confidence. In my experience, those who have sweaty palms have a nervous disposition and may even suffer from a disorder of the nerves. Excessive sweating on the palms should not be ignored and it is advisable to consult a doctor for medical advice. The palms, especially the centre, is connected with the nerve centre in the brain and if this centre is too hollow, in my experience, this indicates great anxiety, causing health problems – hence medical advice should be sought. Extreme anxiety and tensions are generally the root causes of health problems. Statistical research can be done to verify these two observations.

The four basic areas that you should look for while analyzing hands are:
1. type of hand
2. size of hand
3. lines on the hand
4. mounts on the hand

Hands are the chief organs for physical work and are used for gestures and expressions. In our day-to-day life, we often use our hands as form of non-verbal communication. The type of hand, should be the first consideration in palmistry. This indicates the character and personality traits of a person. The setting of the fingers and the manner of opening the palm should be noted next by a palmist. Each finger reveals a different attitude. The tips of the fingers contain the nerve endings of the body. Presuming destiny is stored in the unconscious part of the brain and transmitted through the nerves of the hand, the length, the shape and the markings on the fingers relate to personality and how this builds destiny. Each one of us has a mission in our existence. Sometimes we are not aware of it, but life moves towards it. Mounts and signs on mounts, reveal great secrets of this destiny.

Type of Hand
Look at the hands of the person who plays sports and compare them with one who paints – is the shape of the hands the same? In the same way, compare the hands of a professor with those of a plumber. Hands reveal personality and the type of profession one is likely to follow. I also give a lot of importance to the thumb in my professional readings – the longer it is, the greater are the chances of being successful in life. There has been little statistical research done on this and needs more exploration. There are several different types of hands and they all have different meanings.

Primary Hand
Primary hands are coarse to touch, slightly heavy and non-symmetrical. People with such hands are materially inclined. Daily sustenance, food, clothing and shelter are the focus of their lives. Spirituality or self-realization have little or no meaning. As a general rule, very few lines are seen on such a hand. The length of the thumb is short, barely reaching the base of the first finger, when it is held close to the other fingers. They are the hands of people who have high activity levels. They achieve their goals through sheer hard work.

Square Hand

As the name suggests, the shape of the palm and the tip of the fingers is square in appearance. Persons with this type of hand are practical and level headed. You cannot call such persons quarrelsome, but they can be very fixed and stubborn in their views. Those who are in high administrative positions or in business, have square shaped hands. If the head line on such hands is inclined towards the mount of the moon, the individual may not be artistic in nature, but may still be good collector of art. If the fingers are short and square on a square hand, the person may be a skeptic and have little faith in spirituality. If the fingers are long on a square hand, the person will be very practical and also intellectual. The length of the thumb and the line of head, will decide how successful they will be in life.

Philosopher's Hand

One of the main features of the Philosopher's Hand is that it is long and has fingers with knotty joints. Great philosophers, leaders and intellectuals have such hands. They are not materialistic people but are full of idealism. Generally, the first phalange containing the nail, is longer than the other two phalanges of the finger. These knots may indicate accumulated wisdom, but there is no accumulation of wealth. These could indicate spiritually inclined persons who follow their own path of principles, morals and ethics, and hence it is essential for them to satisfy their inner self rather than the outer physical self. The fear of retribution too, is strong in them. Generally, life for such persons, who follows a path of rightness, is tough. They work more for the good of mankind rather than their own personal desires.

The great Mahatma Gandhi, Abraham Lincoln, and Mother Teresa, are some who possessed this type of hand. Note the long and knotty fingers of the philosopher's hand in photo 3.1, 3.2 and 3.2.

Photo 3.1: Abraham Lincoln
Source:http://lisawallerrogers.files.wordpress.com/2009/06/february-5-1865_-abraham-lincoln1.jpg

Photo 3.2: Photo of Mahatma Gandhi Source:http://www.mynews.in/News/dailyimage/news/indian-hero-mahatma-gandhi.jpg

Photo 3.3: Photo of Mother Teresa
Source:http://www.luisprada.com/Protected/IMAGES/motherteresa.jpg

Artist's Hand

The Artist's Hand is beautifully round shaped, with round tapering fingers. They are full, soft and tender to touch. But it is better for success if the hand is not soft but firm. The colour of the palm is slightly pink. As the name suggests, it is the hand of artistic and creative people. If the Artist's Hand has a good sun line (line below the third finger), the person is likely to become successful by following a creative pursuit. They are guided more by impulse and instinct rather than logic and knowledge. They are moody and temperamental by nature. Good food, good company and good ambience, are equally important in life. If, on such a hand, the headline slopes low towards the mount of the moon, such persons are prone to depression and loneliness. If the headline, the line of the sun and fate, are long and the hand is firm with round tapering fingers, such a person will excel in their artistic endeavors.

Psychic Hand

This hand is probably the most beautiful in appearance. It is long, narrow and slender, with long, pointed fingers. Even the fingernails are long, narrow and almond shaped. Such persons are visionaries. Time and again, it has been seen that those who have breadth of vision and lack practical worldly wisdom, are materially not very successful. Those who possess such beautiful psychic hands may have beautiful souls but may have very difficult lives. They are easily deceived. Psychic hands are the hands of seers, *rishis* and ascetics, who are devotional and religious. They feel and say things through their soul and do not believe in the superficialities of life.

Mixed Hand

Generally, hands are not of any one particular type but a mix of any of the categories above – and have a mix of characteristics too. Persons who possess such a hand are more accommodating and compromising by nature. Desire for change drives them and challenges of life are seen as obstacles to be overcome with hard work and are not looked upon as deterrents.

Size of the Hand

In judging the size of hands, one must bear in mind:
 1. the gender of the person
 2. the height and body weight of the person.

Measure the back of the hand from the wrist to the extremity of the second finger. There are six types of hands depending upon their size.

1. Very Small Hands
Those who have very small hands are generally narrow-minded and suspicious by nature. They have little order in their ideas and actions and generally do not make any contribution to society or mankind.

2. Small Hands
Those who have small hands tend to be lazy though they have big dreams. They have talent, ability and competence, but due to idleness, they do not make great use of their talents.

3. Average Hands
The Average Hands individual is practical and worldly-wise. These people are diplomatic and tactful in their actions and words. They may have moderate imaginations but are practical by nature.

4. Long Hands
Those with Long Hands have analytical talents and the aptitude for minute details. They seek to be useful to society in some way and are generally socially active.

5. Very Long Hands
Individuals with Very Long Hands are overly sensitive and emotional. They live in an imaginary world of their own. They desire to do everything systematically and on time. Strangely, they may not be too happy with their lives and may grumble about work, family, relationships and their daily routine.

Fingers

See Figure 7 for the names of each finger as noted in palmistry. Each finger reveals a different attitude. Fingers that are short in length or set low in the palm, diminishes the attributes associated with that finger and vice-a-versa. Those who have pads on the tips of their fingers (Figure 8), possess a love of beauty and music. Strangely, they have a certain mystical magnetism that draws others towards them, and if they have wheat lines (especially in the shape of an eye), and *Madhura rekha* (Figure 6), on the thumb, (you can read more about lines on the thumb in chapter 2), they possess strong magnetic powers and money. They prosper in life.

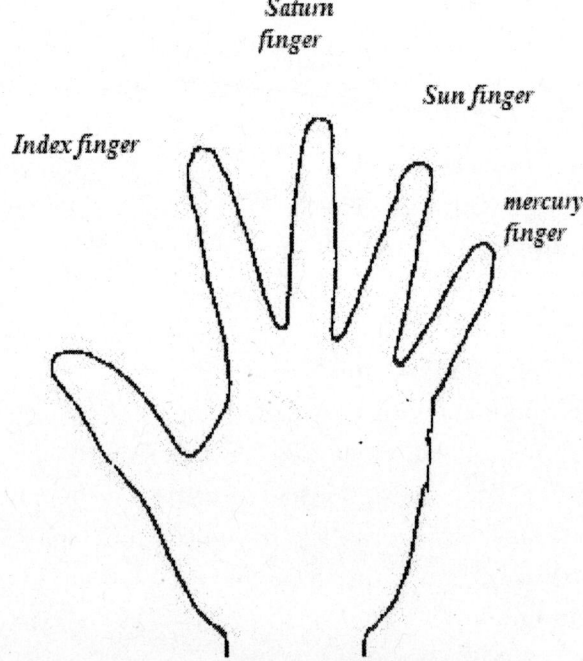

Figure 7: Fingers and their names

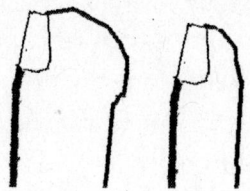

Figure 8: Finger with and without pads

First or Index Finger
The First Finger is also known as the Finger of Jupiter. It is representative of ego and desire for recognition and position in life.

Middle Finger
The Middle Finger is also known as the Finger of Saturn. It is representative of balance of mind, discipline and solitude. Responsibility towards life, work and loved ones, can also be determined by the length, marking and leaning of this finger.

Ring Finger
The Ring Finger is also known as the Apollo finger or the Finger of the Sun. This indicates desire for money, art and fame.

Little Finger
The Little Finger is also known as the Finger of Mercury. It represents communication skills, eloquence and wit. Business acumen and inclination towards scientific research is also determined by this finger.

Mounts

The Mounts of the hands (Figure 9), are the fleshy cushions found at the base of the four fingers and the thumb, as well as at the percussion of the hand. Mounts on the hand are very important in predictions.

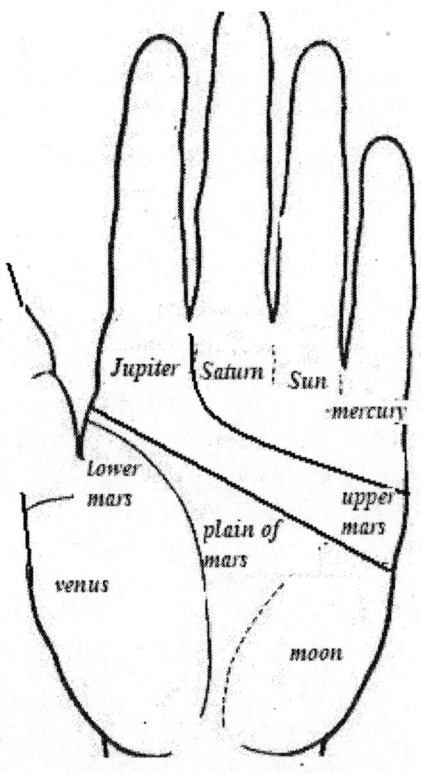

Figure 9: Mounts and their names

Mounts in palmistry
1. Mount of Jupiter – below the index finger
2. Mount of Saturn – below the middle finger
3. Mount of Apollo or the Sun – below the ring finger
4. Mount of Mercury – below the little finger
5. Mount of Venus – below the thumb
6. Mount of the Moon or Luna – opposite the Mount of Venus and alittle above the wrist
7. Lower Mount of Mars – just below the Mount of Jupiter
8. Upper Mount of Mars – between the Mount of Mercury and the Mount of the Moon
9. Plain of Mars – the area in the centre of the palm, though not exactly a mount.

What the meaning of each mount is and how important they are in defining destiny, you can read as examples in the *Hands of the Rich and Famous*, Part II, of this book. Below, is a brief introduction.

1. **Mount of Jupiter** (below the Index finger), indicates leadership qualities – a person's desire to lead others. Position in society, ambitions and ego, are also primarily determined from this mount.

2. **Mount of Saturn** (below the Middle finger), indicates wisdom and a sense of responsibility. Character, analytical powers, and the desire for worldly goods, are also determined by this mount.

3. **Mount of the Sun** (below the Ring finger), indicates desire and love of the fine arts. Optimism and enthusiasm in any person can be determined by this

mount. Worldly desires for fame, name and money, are all determined by this mount.

4. **Mount of Mercury** (below the Little finger), indicates mind and eloquence. The finger also determines bent of mind towards scientific research and business.

5. **Mount of Venus** (below the Thumb), indicates passion and sexual desire. The vitality, generosity and warmth of a person can be determined from this mount.

6. **Mount of the Moon** (below Upper Mars), indicates imagination, travel and the desire for change in a person.

7. **Lower Mars** (below the Mount of Jupiter), indicates the trait of courage.

8. **Upper Mars** (below the Mount of Mercury), indicates a person's patience and tolerance levels.

Plain of Mars (centre of the palm), represents physical and emotional courage.

Part I: IV
THE MEANING OF LINES ON THE PALM

THERE ARE SIX principal lines: Life, Heart, Head, Fate, Sun and Health lines.

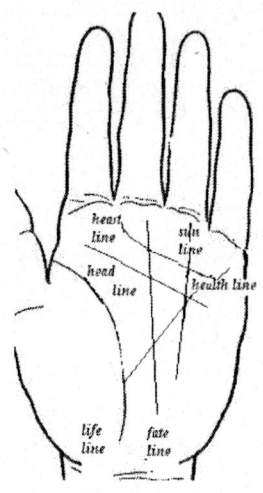

Figure 10: Six principal lines on the palm

Major or Principal Lines

Major or Principal Lines are so called because they hold major portfolios in the cabinet of destiny.

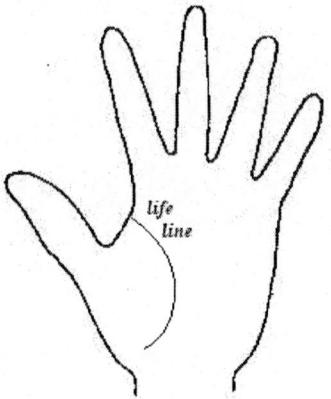

Figure 11: Life Line

Line of Life

The Life Line usually circles the thumb and begins under the mount of Jupiter and extends to the wrist (see Figures 10 & 11). It encircles the thumb and in most cases ends at the base of the hand. All major life events, as well as the health of the person, are indicated by this line. The Line of Life represents the physical capacity and vitality of the person, the possibility of disease and longevity. I would like to add, in my study of palmistry and in my professional experience, I have not yet come across any hand where the Life Line is missing. Fate, Sun, Health or Heart lines may or may not be present in all hands and a single line instead of two separate Head and Heart lines is also possible – however, to have life without having a Life Line is not possible in my experience. A person (you may call it a soul), travels through the journey of life on the track called the Life Line. Every detail is marked on this line, be it happiness, sorrow, travel, illness and disease. It is a kind of scale where readings will be marked and the reasons for these can be found elsewhere on the hand.

Line of Head

The Head Line normally cuts across the palm or curves downward (see Figures 10 & 12). The starting and ending points of this line may differ in different people. It is an indicator of mental faculties, education, intelligence and mental health. The length and the starting and ending points of the Line of Head, all have great significance. You may find it interesting to read the significance of this line in examples of rich and famous given in Part II.

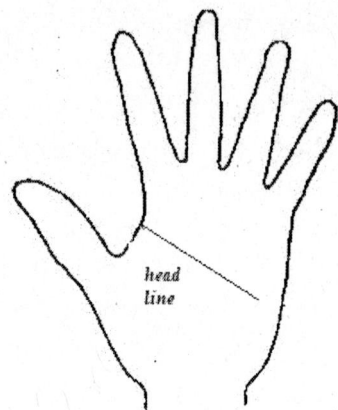

Figure 12: Head Line

Line of Heart

The Heart Line cuts laterally across the upper palm below the first and little finger (see Figures 10 & 13). Note that the starting and ending points of this line may differ individuals.

Love, emotions and functioning of the heart as an organ, can be seen from the Heart Line. If there are bad signs (dot, cross, star, bar, break) on the Heart Line, a threat to life is possible. In ancient Hindu palmistry, longevity was judged from the Heart Line. But should palmists assess longevity from the Heart Line in the present era when medical science has advanced? **The death rate from heart disease is dropping** and medical science has greatly reduced the risks of death caused by heart disease – for which we should be thankful. Has modern science then negated this ancient theory of palmistry?

A heart attack occurs when a blood vessel to the heart becomes blocked. With blockage, not enough blood reaches that part of the heart muscle and permanent damage results. Heart failure is a chronic condition in which the heart cannot pump blood properly. It does not mean that the heart suddenly stops working. Heart failure develops over a period of years. Now, check on the Heart Line for black or bluish dot/s – these indicate blockages, but heart failure only occurs when there is a complete break in the Heart Line. Presence of a star and a break on the Heart Line (see Figure 13.1), indicates serious heart failure affecting longevity. The health of the heart is linked to health and longevity. Blue, red or black dots and a branch line falling from the Heart Line – all these are indications of heart problems where medical intervention and adopting a healthier lifestyle may help. But when there is a sign of a star followed by a break on the Heart Line, it may prove fatal.

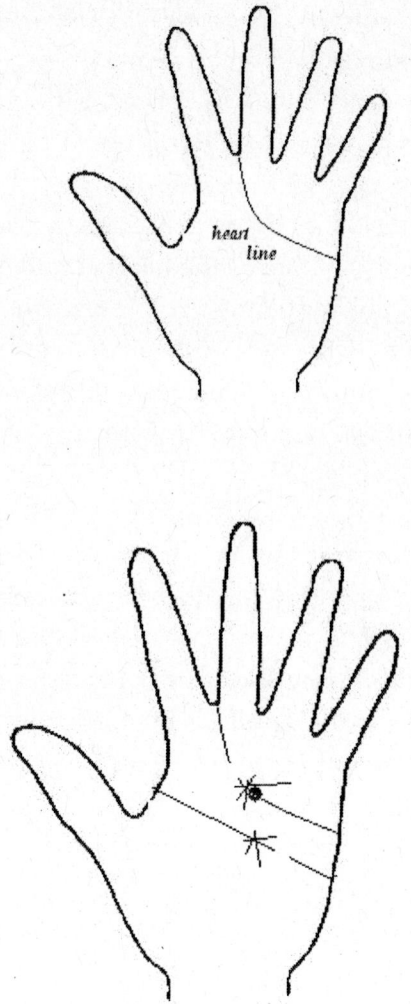

Figure 13: Line of the Heart; Figure 13.1: Signs on Heart and Head Lines affecting longevity

When a person's heart stops, he/she can be put onto a ventilator. Medically, a patient is 'alive' while on a vent. I propose no single sign on any Line be seen for conclusive results – also check the Head Line. If the Heart Line and Head Line both have complete breaks or a star, this can be a conclusive sign for checking longevity. Those patients who are medically brain dead are still are considered to be alive – but only as long as the heart circulates blood in the body. When the ventilator is removed from a brain dead patient, the patient may never take another breath from that moment on and at that point if there are no signs of respiration or any heartbeat, then the person can medically be declared to be dead.

I further propose, in addition to the Life Line, the Heart and Head Lines together, be checked for longevity. In my studies and research, a break and star signs on the Heart and Head Lines, can be considered reliable checks affecting longevity. The Life Line, of course, will always show lifespan, but these two lines seen together are also good indicators of lifespan.

Line of Fate

The Line of Fate is also known as the Line of Money or Career. This line runs vertically from the middle of the base of the palm and up towards the middle finger (see Figures 10 & 14). Note that the starting and ending points of this line may differ in individuals. This line indicates money, wealth, growth, financial and professional gains and losses. Changes, both financial and professional, are also indicated by this line. It indicates the possibility of gaining material wealth, as well as love and marriage.

Figure 14: Fate Line

Line of the Sun

Line of the Sun is a vertical line and may begin anywhere on the palm, but will end at the mount below the third or Ring finger. It is also called the Line of Fame or the Line of Brilliance – and to it has been ascribed the gift of great artistic talents, wealth and fame (see Figures 10 & 15). It is possible that some people may not possess this line at all. It represents success of one's efforts – whether in the acquisition of wealth, politics, acting, love, travel or sport.

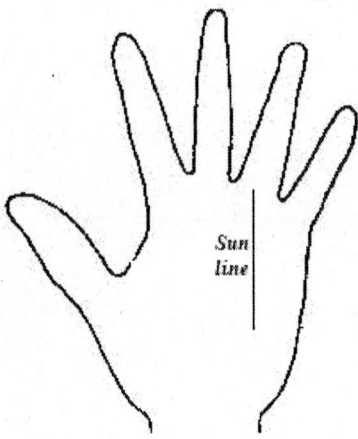

Figure 15: Line of the Sun

Line of Health

The Line of Health rises from or just below the Mount of Mercury and goes down the hand towards the Life Line. Ideally, the Health Line should not touch the Life Line. It represents health and disease. If the line is steady, clear and does not actually touch the Life Line, it is a good sign and better still if the Health Line is totally absent. Absence of this on the hand means good health, with no major illness or disease throughout life. If it is broken, it denotes ill-health. If broken into distinct pieces, it denotes severe illness related to the digestive system or liver problems.

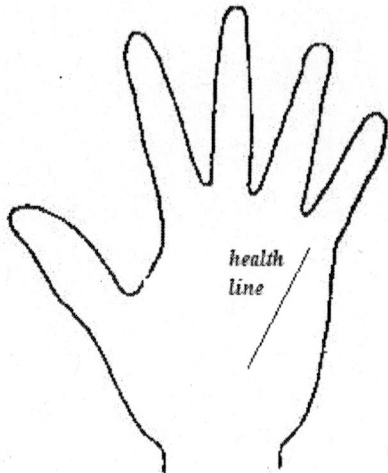

Figure 16: Line of Health

Ancient palmists correlated success in career with health line. Many statistical studies have also shown correlation between health and career. So, a clear well defined

Health Line indicates logical reasoning and good health, plus a good career, while a broken up mercury line indicates confused thinking and indifferent health affecting one's career (see Figure 10 & 16).

Other Lines:

Line of Intuition

The Line of Intuition forms a half circle from the Mount of Mercury to the Mount of the Moon. If present in a hand (not always the case), this line represents the intellectual and imaginative faculties of mind. The person may have vivid dreams. It denotes extreme sensitiveness. Such a person is gifted with intuition and the faculty of clairvoyance (see Figure 17).

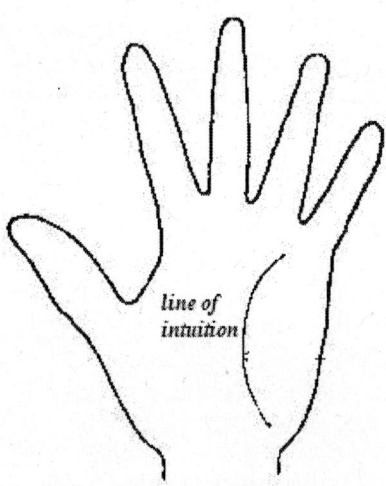

Figure 17: Line of Intuition

Girdle of Venus

The Girdle of Venus is a semicircular line rising between the first and second fingers, and ending between the third and fourth. Sometimes this girdle forms a complete ring around the base of the fingers. This line denotes a nervous temperament and passionate nature (see figure 18). An exaggerated and strong Girdle of Venus denotes a great passionate force which may eventuate in carnal gratification. It is common for this line to be missing on the hand. The absence of the line means a person with a calm character who is able to control his/her feelings.

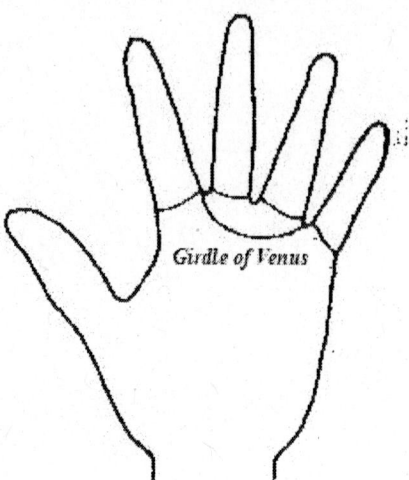

Figure 18: Girdle of Venus

Bracelets

Bracelets are also called Rascettes. Bracelets form the chain-like lines at the base of the hand on the wrist. They are merely signs of health. It is most common to have two or three bracelets. It is possible, though rare, that some people may have only one bracelet, or more than three bracelets. People who live to a moderate age usually have one bracelet and in those who have more than three bracelets, it denotes a very long and prosperous life. If any bracelet is broken, this indicates ill health (see Figure 19). In Hindu palmistry, having four bracelets is considered very lucky and indicates opulence and riches in life.

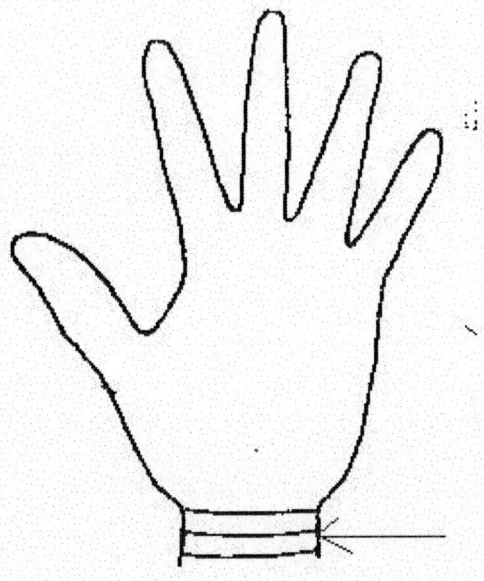

Figure 19: Bracelets

Line of Mars

The Line of Mars runs parallel to the Line of Life, on the Lower Mount of Mars and/or the Mount of Venus (see Figure 20). The length of this line can vary. It corrects many of the breaks and defects in the Line of Life. This line is not necessarily present in all hands. If present, it represents protection and a vital force. This line offers greater power of resistance to withstand any disease or unexpected shock in life.

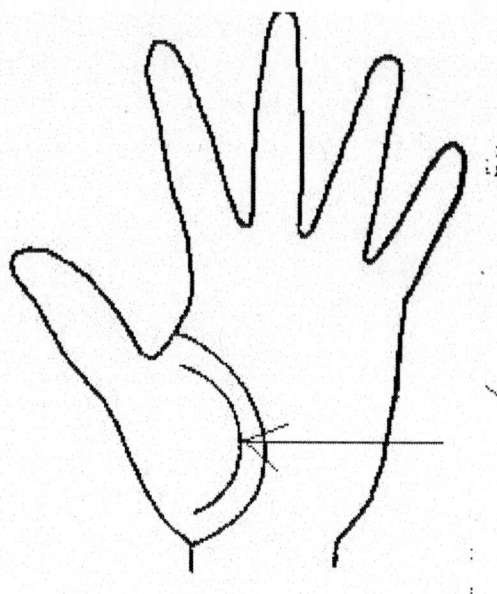

Figure 20: Line of Mars

Line of Marriage

I have written a complete chapter on love, marriage and relationships. In present times, when live-in or co-habitation is common, the Line of Marriage may also be called the Line of Affection or Relationship. Marriage can be indicated by different lines on the palm, but one place I would like to mention, is at the side of the hand below the Mount of Mercury and above the Line of the Heart (see Figure 21). This line represents love relationships and attachments of the heart. When this line lies close to the heart line, the marriage will occur at an early age. When it is near the centre of the mount, the person will be married between ages 25-30, and when it appears near the top of the mount, marriage may occur after 35 years of age. When the line curves upwards, there may be no marriage at all or there may be great discord in marriage.

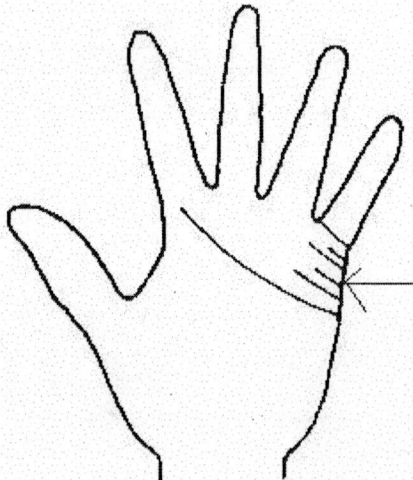

Figure 21: The arrow shows the Line of Marriage or Relationships

Line of Children

The lines for children are small vertical lines on the mount of mercury, at the side of the hand above the Line of Marriage. These lines indicate the possibility of having children and may also indicate the number of children the person is likely to have. Generally, these lines are very fine, hence you may need a fine magnifying lens and good light to see them. Ancients believed that broad and deep lines were for male children and light, faint lines were for female children. Clearly marked lines indicate strong and healthy children (see Figure 22). Lines on the Mount of Venus, close to the thumb, are also lines for children. Note that there will be many such lines but only lines close to thumb are for children.

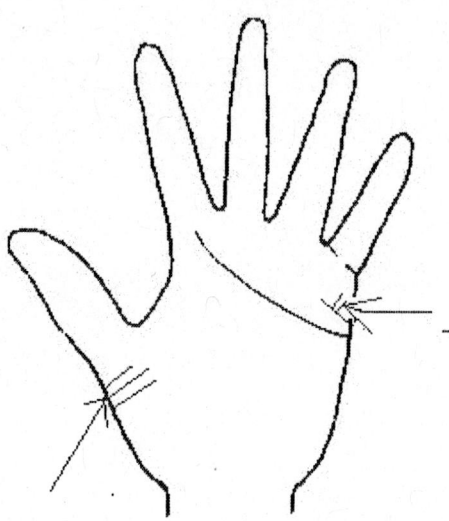

Figure 22: The arrow shows the Lines of Children

Travel lines

Travel can also be seen from many places on the hand. The horizontal lines on the Mount of the Moon are also called Lines of travel (see Figure 23). Small hairlines that leave the line of life towards the mount of the Moon, are also travel lines. Sometimes the short lines that join the fate line from the Mount of Moon also suggest travel.

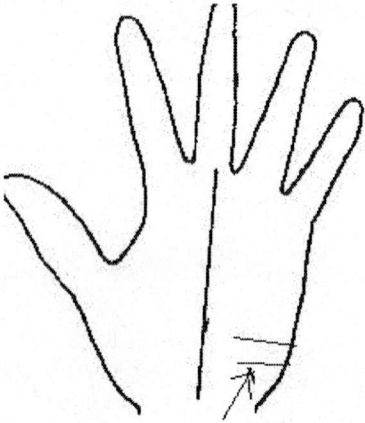

Figure 23: The arrow shows the Line of Travel

Part I: V
LOVE MARRIAGE & RELATIONSHIPS

THE LINE OF THE HEART (Figures 10 & 13), as the name suggests, relate to matters of heart, love and the emotions. Feelings and emotions can be seen from this line and not physical and sensual relationships. If this line runs straight across the palm, as shown in figure 5.1, such a person is generally very giving in love and invests energy in relationships. As per Hindu philosophy, whenever we are too attached to anything or anyone on this earth, there are generally setbacks – meaning that when we lose ourselves and our personality, for our love, relationships and desires, then there is generally more emotional suffering. We can merge but not lose our own personality and identity in the pursuit of love. Emotions and relationships are given more importance in life by a person whose Heart Line runs straight across the palm. Famous Indian filmstar, Aishwarya Rai Bachchan, has a straight Heart Line (see photo and Figure 5.1). Such a person is very emotionally giving in life.

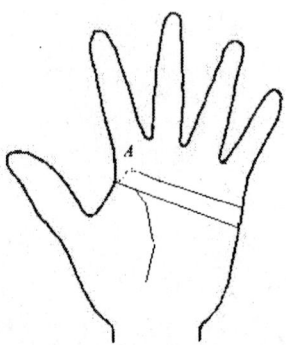

Figure 5.1: The straight Line of Heart

*source:http://indianpalmreading.freeforum.me.uk/celebs-amazing-palms-f11/
aishwarya-rai-bachchan-t343.htm*

When this straight heart line bends and touches the Head and Life Line at a single point, then affection and love is invested in the wrong person (see dotted line in Figure 5.1). A person is more balanced in emotions when it runs and ends between the first and second fingers (see Figure 5.2). However, when this line ends at any point below the second finger (see dotted line B), the person is more self-centred and emotionally less giving or extremely obsessive in love. When there are small hair-like fine lines rising or falling from the Heart Line, it generally denotes infatuation, flirtations, mushy or sometimes sad emotions, but no serious relationships.

It is natural for a human being to feel attraction and emotions if the Heart Line is thin and devoid of these little lines. Such a person is probably cold, stiff, manipulating and emotionally reserved. Whenever there is any break, cut, sign of the star or cross on this line, this shows disorder in the workings of heart as an organ. It is best to adopt a healthy diet and lifestyle and get medical advice if you have any such sign on your Heart Line. Date, time and age can be read on this line, for such afflictions. This line begins below the little finger. The segment of line below each finger is approximately twenty years and the gap between two fingers is ten years each. Hence you can calculate the age when you may have heart problems or emotional attachments, from this line.

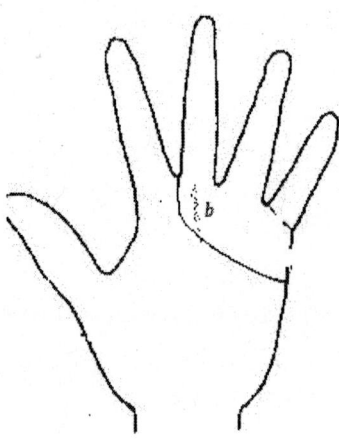

Figure 5.2: The Line of Heart run between the fingers and below the second finger

If the Heart Line ends in a sign that is similar to a fang of a snake (mark of *rahu*), in the south node of the moon, there are generally sorrows from relationships (see Figure 5.3.1), but if it is a sign of V (the mark of *Lord Vishnu*), it is considered very lucky in ancient Hindu palmistry (see Figure 5.3.2). You can read more about the V mark in the section, *Signs on the thumb in Hindu Palmistry*, chapter 2.

There is fine difference between the two signs; the fang is slightly twisted and curved, whereas the V mark of Vishnu has a perfect straight like the alphabet V. In Hindu mythology, the mouth of the snake is symbolic of Eternal Time (*kaal*), which engulfs all human beings from birth to death and is the journey of a soul on earth. No human being can expect only happy experiences, no matter how rich, powerful or famous, they are. It is *kaal* or the Eternal Law, by which we who are born on this earth, experience both ups and downs in our lives. That is probably why the mouth of sthe nake is symbolic of Eternal Time in Hindu mythology. Having this sign of *rahu* on the Heart Line brings both love and sorrow. It surely brings love, but one is attracted to the wrong people who bring sorrow and disappointments in life. Who can say whether Scottish poet, Alfred, Lord Tennyson was right or wrong when he wrote: *Tis better to have loved and lost / Than never to have loved* at all. However, if this line is found at the very start (in childhood), below the little finger, this indicates health problems at that age – also wealth and prosperity to the grandfather.

The sign of V on the Heart Line is considered lucky in matters of love and relationships. In the *Puranas*, a soul that has paid for his/her past sins will have positive *karma* to take forward into his/her next birth. Such a person, will possess this sign on the hand. The trident sign, sign of the *trishul*, also means the same. The possessor of such signs on the Heart Line (V and trident), will attract positive people who will guide them in their times of need – soul mates. If there are other positive signs on the palm, they may marry their soul mate. And though soul mates may or may not be husband and wife, they will surely be companions – to hold one's hands when one needs strength or support in life.

If the Heart Line is the most prominent line in colour and depth, of all lines on the palm, this shows a loving disposition. Such persons make good soul healers, missionaries and social workers. The Heart Line only tells us about the functioning of the heart as an organ and capabilities to love and feel emotions. For marriage and relationships, we need to look at many other signs.

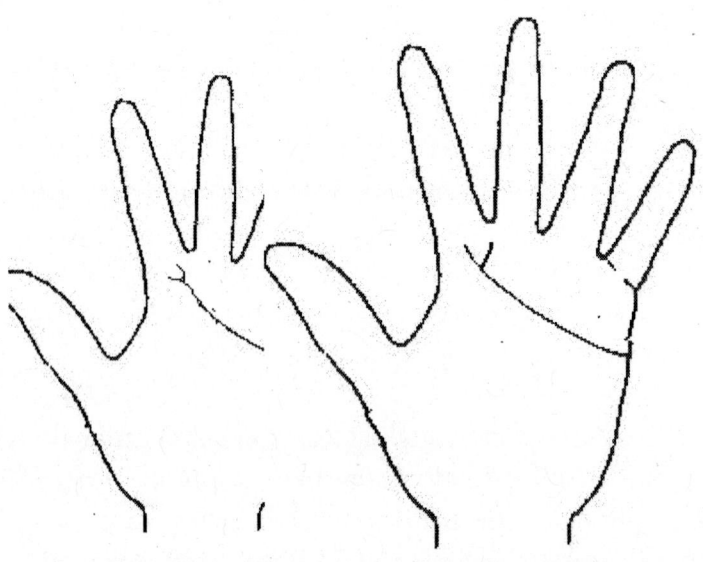

Figure 5.3.1: Mark of Rahu – the south node of the moon;
Figure 5.3.2: V Mark

Let us first ask the question: What is Marriage? Let me try to answer this question and then talk of marriage in palmistry. The meeting of two souls, physically or emotionally, is a relationship, and when given the sanctity of society (or stamp of law), this relationship becomes a marriage. What may be socially acceptable in America may not, however, be accepted in India. Different environments bring variations in thought. Marriage is a ceremony performed for two individuals with the sanctity of social customs and law. Marriage has a strong correlation to era, culture, country, caste, religion, faith – and statisticians can give other factors – but broadly speaking, it is man-made and relationships are God-made (let us call it Destiny).

So what I infer, from my professional experience, is that the deeper the lines are, the longer the duration of the relationship, where couples face the ups and downs of life together. Bad signs (I will discuss later), would infer separation. Shorter and thinner lines can be read as paths of souls crossing each other like ships in the night. Some souls may enter your life to fulfill and complete you, while others may leave you vulnerable and wounded. This is how palmistry can help you, without moral preaching, to understand how each soul has to undergo the process of evolution and enlightenment. Some lessons and wisdom we are born with and some we acquire in our lifetime. Understanding this and moving on is called LIFE.

The first place to look for marriage/relationship is under the little finger above the Heart Line (see Figure 5.3.3(a)). Faint, thin and short lines on this mount indicate infatuation, crushes or college romances. The darker, longer and stronger lines are the probability of marriage. In a marriage line ending like a snake's fang, line of *rahu* – the north node of the moon – the couple may continue to live together but will have separate, individual lives. If the marriage line curves downwards and touches the Line of the Heart, it brings sorrows, even death of the spouse. However, if this line curves upwards towards the fingers, the person may not marry at all. If there is a legal divorce, it generally brings with it a lot of bitterness into the lives of the partners. Curving of the Marriage Line downwards, upwards, a break or sign of an island, brings a lot of sadness into the life of the person.

However, if a curved Marriage Line ends in a cross or a star on the Mount of Mars near the thumb, physical danger, due to the jealous and obsessive nature of the spouse, is possible. A Marriage Line cutting the Line of the Sun would mean separation but with public scandal, bringing disgrace. A happy union between two souls is Destiny, but moving on in life without bitterness is Destiny with enlightenment of soul. We can learn so much from bad situations and bad people. Probably they also have their own task of learning from our lives and for this purpose our destiny paths cross.

The person/s who brings unhappiness into our lives will, like us, die some day, so why spoil today for someone who will not be there tomorrow – why not make today the most important. Probably, the Almighty wrote our destiny in our hands for us to read this map and evolve as better human beings – evolving as better people is the most important thing in the present era of hatred, insecurity and uncertainty.

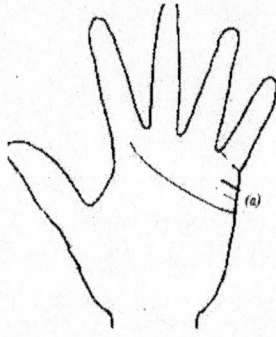

Figure 5.3.3: Marriage/Relationship Lines

The next place to look for marriage is the thumb. I have already emphasized the importance of the markings on the thumb in palmistry (chapter 2). Vertical lines, *kesar rekha* (Figure 6/ Line 7), indicates happiness. This is a very important line, since marriage, career or money has no meaning unless you derive contentment and happiness first. It is possible for you to get married, acquire wealth and have a respectable career but still feel the void of missing joy in your heart.

Rati Rekha (Figure 6/ Line 5), indicates marriage or relationships. Whenever there are subsidiary lines above or below this line, it means more than one marriage or relationship. Confirm the same from the Wheat Line (Figure 6 / line 1). If this line too is broken or has fork, it means more than one relationship and the time of separation can be read from the Wheat Line. An island on the *Rati Rekha* (Figure 5.3.4), means clashes due to differences of opinion between the couple or it may mean extra marital affairs, if there are subsidiary line/s on either spouse's thumb.

Now observe and understand (Figure 5.3.5) – the mark of the fish. It is very similar to an island, but in complete contrast, means growth and prosperity after marriage (or relationship). There may be a bitter legal divorce if a small vertical line divides this line or there is a small black spot on this line. A single deep vertical line from the baseline of the thumb, cutting this line, would mean legal problems that the couple may have to face due to other situations or persons. If this line is very fragmented, the person may not marry at all.

Figure 5.3.5 Sign of the Island
Figure 5.3.5: Sign of the Fish
Figure 5.3.6: Sign of the Dot

No one line can give a complete answer and confirmation. If marriage is indicated on the Mount of Mercury/ thumb, it can be corroborated from the Fate Line. The next place to look for signs of marriage is when an Influence line joins the Fate Line (Figure 5.3.7 A).

If there is the sign of an island (Figure 5.3.7 B), or break, (Figure 5.3.7 A), there may be problems after marriage. However, if there is rising line (Figure 5.3.7 C), there will be growth and prosperity after marriage, and change in destiny is indicated by the overlapping of lines (Figure 5.3.7 E).

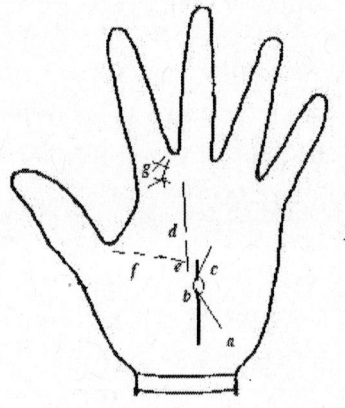

Figure 5.3.7: Marriage Signs on the Fate Line

If a rising line (C), is stronger and slightly broader than the Fate Line, one's financial and social status improves after marriage. At the point where the Influence line touches the Fate Line, the time of marriage (or relationship) can be calculated. If you draw an imaginary line (Figure 5.3.7 F), from inside the base of the thumb to the Fate Line, it can be read as age 22, and the point where fate line touches the Head Line can be read as age 35. Accordingly, calculate the time of marriage by equally dividing the line segment between ages 22 and 35.

One of the best signs for great happiness and prosperity in marriage, is when you have a rising line C on the Fate Line, *Kesar Rekhas* on the thumb and the Sign of the

Cross on the Mount of Jupiter. The Sign of the Cross and the Sign of the Star, especially if joined with a ray (Figure 5.3.7 G), indicates marriage to a person of a higher social order and better economic position. If this cross is nearer the fingers like in G, it means that the person enters later in life or in the twilight years. And if the sign (G), is on top of the Mount of Jupiter, it denotes the middle years of life between 30 to 45; and if below the Mount of Jupiter, it means meeting Mr/Miss Right early in life.

Readers may be familiar with the attributes of Venus – the planet of beauty, love and passion. Now let me explain how to read marriage from the Mount of Venus. The third phalange of the thumb encircled by the Life Line, is the Mount of Venus – the area of love and marriage. The line separating the thumb from the Mount of Venus, *Malika Rekha* (chapter 2, Figure 6 / Line 6), and the Mount of Venus, should both be studied for marriage and relationships. *Malika Rekha*, if in relation to other lines on the thumb appears very dark, thick and coarse, then it is not considered lucky for marriage.

If this line, along with the Wheat Line and *Rati* line, is cut in the middle by a vertical line, there are problems in marriage, even legal complications. For happiness in life, look for *Kesar Rekhas* on the thumb. If there is the Sign of the Cross (X) or the Sign of Plus (+) on the centre of the broad area (nucleus of the ridges), of the first phalange of the thumb, then physical satisfaction will be missing in marriage, but it is possible husband and wife may otherwise share an amicable relationship.

The Mount of Venus is actually the third phalange of the thumb. To check for this, try twisting or turning your thumb from the base – the portion on the palm that moves along with this movement is the Mount of Venus. If the Mount of Venus is high, such a person possesses SA and is passionate. An over-developed or under-developed Mount generally brings disappointment in love. A person is of a worrying and nervous disposition if there are many criss-cross lines on this Mount. The line running from the Life Line on the Mount of Venus (Figure 5.3.8 A), indicates marriage or relationship. Relationships become stronger if this line (A), runs close to the Life Line. The level of affection may vary and end with this line.

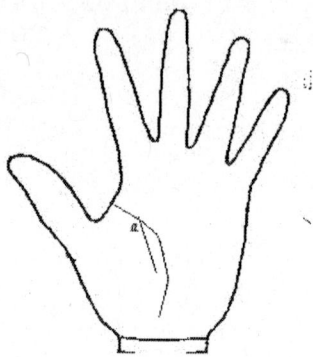

Figure 5.3.8: Marriage signs on Mount of Venus

The person/s you love may not just be your spouse but also your soul mate, if this line is as thick and dark as the Life Line, or throws a branch towards the Life Line. However, if this branch cuts the Fate Line the union will bring disgrace and financial loss. An island is seen on this line if the person is involved in a guilty or extramarital affair (Figure 5.3.9. B).

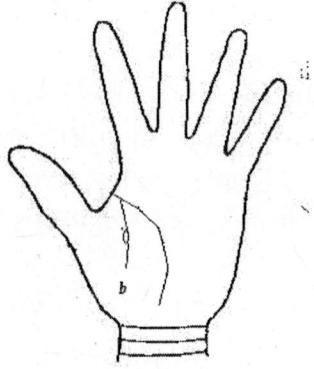

Figure 5.3.9: Island on Relationship Line, Mount of Venus

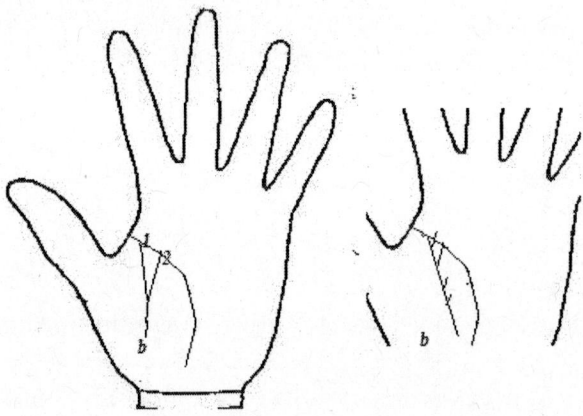

Figure 5.3.10: Relationship Sign 1, 2 on Mount of Venus
Figure 5.3.10a: Rising lines on Relationship Line

See points 1 and 2 in Figure 5.3.10: the Relationship Line is in shape of a Y; points 1 and 2 on the Life Line are different time periods, but the person you love is the same. The line ends in a star or a cross if the love of your life dies.

In my own personal observation, I have noticed a second line running close to the Life Line, having rising lines (Figure 5.3.10a), indicating that the husband and wife are not only married to each other but may also be professional business partners. Rising lines are actually growth and prosperity lines in business after marriage. The complete hand should always be read for definite and accurate predictions.

PART I: VI
MONEY & CAREER

IN THIS MATERIAL world, our career and money goals become the goals of our lives – we spend our entire lifetimes in pursuit of these goals and are unhappy if we are unable to achieve them. How ironic! Do we actually feel fulfilled when we achieve them? Do we feel we have achieved the purpose of our life?

We live in a world of illusion – *maya* – where we are all running a race and have no time to think what we actually want, rather than what is expected from us. Professional success, power, money and fame are probably the only barometers by which we measure the growth of a person, hence we all run in this pursuit of high ratings on this barometer. When we learn to read professional growth and success through palmistry, we first need to understand that over and above us, there probably exists a Law of Destiny. We may or may not have control over destiny (endless debate!), but we definitely have control over how we react towards it. The day we learn to take professional ups and downs with equanimity, we will, to a great extent, attain *nirvana*. Success, money or fame do not enslave us, but our ignorance does. Knowledge (*Gyan Yoga*), spirituality (*Bhakti Yoga*) and actions (*Karma Yoga*), are probably the only means to fulfillment.

Scientists estimate that the storage capacity of the human brain is infinite and no limits exist. Then why is it difficult to assume that the passive, unconscious part of brain has stored information about our Destiny?

On the palm, the Line of Fate (Figures 10 & 14), and the thumb, tell us about success and failure, and when we meet obstacles or opportunities. The shape of the hand, its texture and the colour of palm and well-developed mounts, should be noticed first. If the mounts are well-developed and there are positive signs on them, even if Fate Line is missing, the person will certainly gain success. In my experience, I have seen the Fate Line missing on the hands of even those who are born in affluent families and have the luxuries of life without making there own personal contribution. Such persons enjoy riches but there may be no excitement, adventure or purpose in their lives. Hardships in life strengthen the soul and help us evolve as better human beings – since this evolution of soul is missing, the Fate Line too, is missing on the hands of some, born into riches. In my experience, hard times teach us more than good times, so the missing Fate Line on such hands means life with no real challenges.

If the Fate Line starts from the wrist and goes up to the base of the second finger, such a person achieves success no doubt, but is very focused and self-centred in his personality. If this line runs very close to the Life Line, the person's family dictates or holds power over professional choices. Such a person is hindered in displaying his own personality in his work, hence disillusionment follows in life. In India, I have seen this line on the hands of daughters who submit to the will of the family and also on the hands of those who are engaged in the family business with brothers and other family members as business partners – and do not have much say in the important decisions of their own lives (Figure 6.1a). On the contrary, if the Fate Line starts from the Mount of the Moon, away from the Life line, family ties do not hold him/her back and such a person generally makes his destiny in a land away from his birth or travels frequently (Figure 6.1b). A Fate Line starting from the wrist and ending near the base of second finger, a line from the Mount of the Moon joining this line, can be read as the period of marriage (Chapter 5), or growth opportunities in foreign lands.

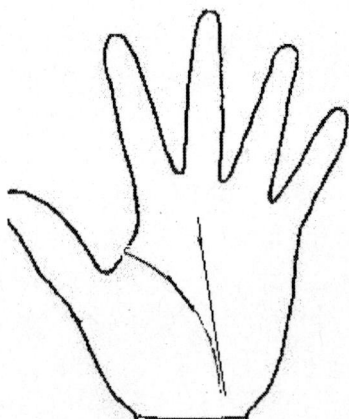

Figure 6.1a: Fate Line running close to the Life Line

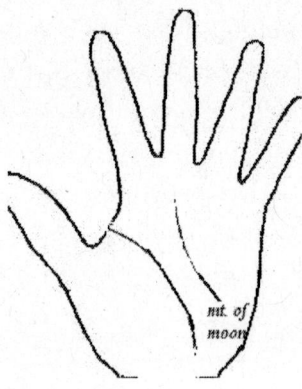

Figure 6.1b: Fate Line running close to the Life Line

If the Fate Line starts from the middle of the palm and runs to the base of the second finger, such a person is self-made and meets his destiny after overcoming obstacles and struggles early in life. Just as the starting point of a Fate Line is important, so is the ending point. The period after 35 years is full of hardships and struggles, if the Fate Line ends before reaching the Head Line. The thickness and colour of the Fate Line should always be considered. A very dark, broad or very thin Fate Line is not lucky. There may be many struggles and hardships even for basic existence. The importance of money cannot be negated – without money life can be like running on a treadmill – such a soul may have lots to learn in his journey of life to rise above daily existence and still be able to maintain his inner equilibrium (Figure 6.2, Line A).

When the Fate Line stops at the Heart Line (Figure 6.2, Line B), love and relationships are generally the reasons for one's professional fall. If there are negative signs on the Heart Line, functioning of the heart may also be affected. The space between the Head and Heart Lines cover the age from 35 to 55. I calculate age in this space by dividing the line segment and age. For instance, calculating the center of this line segment between the Head and Heart Lines would give age: (35+55) / 2= 45. Dividing the line segment would give age: (35+45) / 2 = 40.

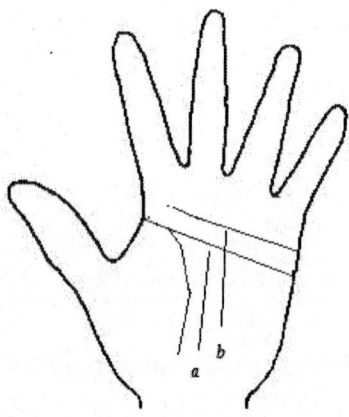

Figure 6.2: Starting points of the Fate Line

If a Fate Line, instead of ending near the base of the second finger, turns towards the base of the third finger or even sends a branch towards third finger, such a person attains great name and fame in his lifetime. The third or ring finger is the finger of the Sun or the finger of great fame. The line that runs towards the third finger is the LIne of the Sun. The long and straight Line of the Sun gives creative talent. Such a person acquires name and fame because of creative talent. Strong Sun and Fate Lines and favorable signs on the thumb, bring great fortune and fame, owing to the creative talents of the person (see Chapter 12: plate of the famous singer Michael Jackson's hand, for a strong Sun Line). Singers, musicians and actors also have well-developed Mounts of Venus. The Line of Jupiter, when found (as in hand of Michael Jackson), gives social status and respectability, along with creative talent. Professional ups and downs can be seen from the Fate Line. A long thumb and straight Head Line, gives a person will power and intelligence to overcome obstacles in life.

An unusually long thumb, long little finger, and powerful Fate Line, Sun Line and Line of Jupiter (starting from the Life Line), have made Barrack Obama into President of the most powerful nation in the world (see photo 7). The Line of Jupiter gives power and position and a strong long little finger gives eloquence.

Sometimes, the Line of Fate moving towards the second finger suddenly turns or bends towards the first finger – such a person attains a position of great power in his/her lifetime (see Photo 8 of former President and present Prime Minister of Russia, Vladmir Putin).

If, the first phalange of the second finger is long and has the Sign of a Cross over it, professional worries are usually immense (Figure 6.5 Sign a), and if there is a sign like an eye of a lens on the second segment/phalange of the second finger, professional growth and happiness can be seen (Figure 6.5 Sign b). Note the Zodiac sun sign of Capricorn is located on the first phalange of the second finger; Aquarius on the second phalange; and Pisces on the third phalange. Capricorn in astrology is the natural ruler of career; Aquarius rules gains and fulfillment of desires, and Pisces rules expenditure.

Signs of the flag, tree or trident (see chapter 2, section *Signs on the Thumb in Hindu Palmistry*), on fingers or on the Mount of Saturn, are considered lucky for career and money, whereas, the signs of the star, *rahu*-like shape of a a serpent and cross, are not favourable, as given by ancient Hindu palmistry.

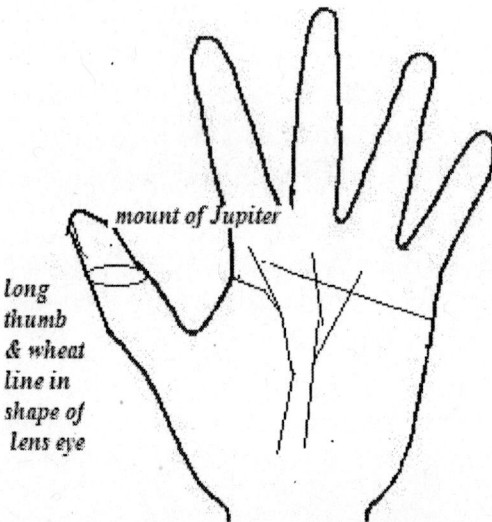

Figure 6.3: Signs of power on the hand

If the Fate Line enters and ends in the second finger, it is not considered favourable. In my experience, it means that work becomes more of a burden and a duty and less imbued with passion. I have also seen that in women, it means some kind of familial responsibilities that they cannot shirk or move away from due to their moral binding.

Figure 6.4: Thick club-like thumb

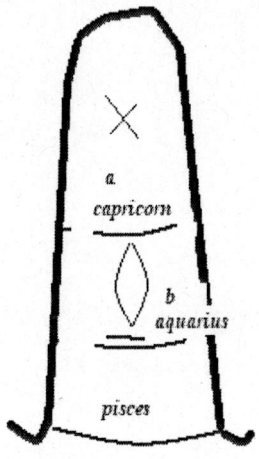

Figure 6.5: Second finger

If there is an island sign, like a grain of wheat, on the Fate Line, there may be financial and professional woes.

However, if there is the sign of a fish, there will be financial abundance and growth (Figure 6.6). Note the difference of signs: line A has the sign of an island and line B that of a fish.

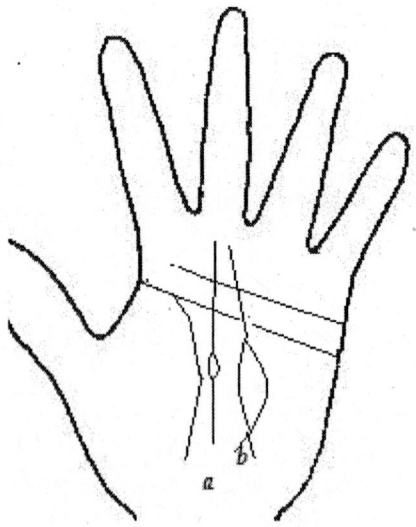

Figure 6.6: Fate Line a & b
a = island sign; b = fish sign

If, there are bars on the Fate Line, it can be interpreted as a tough period in career growth, when obstacles have to be overcome to achieve success. If the Fate Line runs straight but has the sign of an island, cross, bars, star or breaks, it will do us good to understand through palmistry, that life presents some challenges but only in certain phases of life – and during these phases, through strong will power and mental strength, one can overcome and finally be the winner! Life has, and will always have, different phases, but no phase remains forever. One may not be able change one's destiny but one can change how one reacts to it. If there is a complete break, this means huge loss, but if any second line begins before the line ends, this means there will be career changes.

The most important signs are the ones at the end of the Fate Line: negative signs (star, cross, break, bars), mean ill luck follows the person throughout life; and favorable signs (trident, flag, tree, triangle, square, fish, M or W), means that luck favours one throughout life. If there are some lines running parallel to the Fate Line – they too bring luck (supporting lines), but these lines should not be too close to the Fate Line (axe lines) – that would mean hurdles at every corner (see Figure 6.7 to understand the difference).

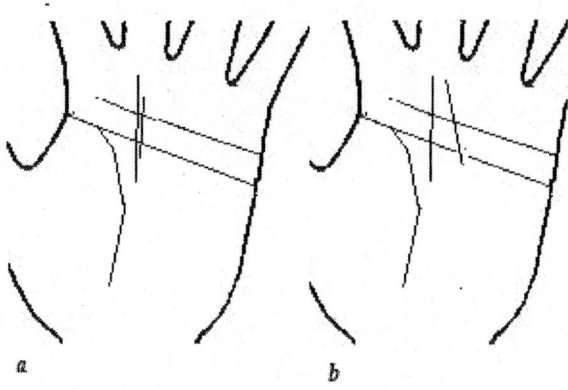

Figure 6.6: Fate Line
a = axe line; b = supporting line

After reading the Fate Line, the next place to read career and money is the thumb (Figure 6, Lines 1 & 6). I have found the reading amazingly accurate and whenever anyone opens his/her palm, my eyes first see the Wheat Line to read the social and economic status of the person.

To calculate age on Line 1, the Wheat Line or *Pushpa Rekha*, should be thought of as consisting of three equal parts and the middle of this line would be age 38 (Figure 6.7).

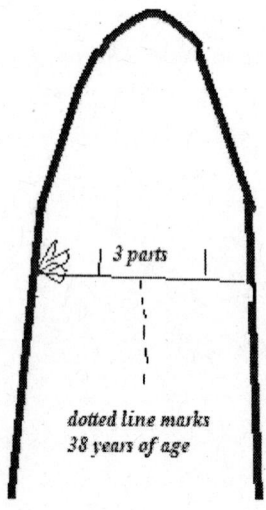

Figure 6.7: Age on thumb and sign of the flower

The shape of the Wheat Line is very important in predicting growth and prosperity in life. If this is in a straight line with dents or broken in its course, it implies struggles and hardships. Dents and breaks imply change or setbacks in social and economic status. But if there are two parallel straight lines of equal length, it means riches and prosperity.

The sign of the mouth of a serpent, *rahu*, anywhere on this line, is not favourable and there may be some unhealthy competition or secret adversaries at work. A line beginning with negative signs (cuts, crosses, star), but later takes the shape of a grain of wheat, then money and riches follow initial hardships in life. It is lucky to have a Wheat Line in the shape of a fish. Great professional growth and money is predicted. A Wheat Line in the shape of a flower with petals, anywhere on the line (Figure 6.7), gives great social status, and if this sign is distinct, it may give political career and position. Subsidiary lines to the main Wheat Line always means growth opportunities and changes for betterment in life.

The complete hand should be seen by a palmist, not just one sign, and with experience one learns to read the hand like a book. I always studying a hand as fascinating and as mysterious as any book of suspense.

The next place to read career and money on the palm are in the mounts. The Mount of Saturn and the Line of Fate running towards this mount, below the second finger, are most important to look for career and money. Negative signs (star, cross, bars, island, and mole/dot) on this mount, bring constant struggle and obstacles in professional life. Good signs (trident, triangle, fish, flag, and tree), bring amazing success. I have already written about the Mount of Saturn and the Fate Line running towards it. Let us study the other mounts on the hand.

The Mount of Jupiter, just below the first finger, gives political career, position, power and social status. When reading hands for professional growth, length, width, starting and ending points of the Head Line, should all be carefully noted. The Line of the Sun and Fate, are good indicators of professional growth whereas a strong Head Line starting from the Mount of Jupiter, plus a strong thumb, gives great social status and power. Such a person attains a position of power irrespective of his/her birth. See Part II for photos of the hands of Barrack Obama and Sonia Gandhi – both have long thumbs and Head Lines starting from the Mount of Jupiter (Figure 6.3).

I call the mount of Jupiter, the Mount of Power. This mount, when high and balanced by strong lines of head and thumb, takes you to the seat of power – no matter how humble your beginnings. If the Mount of Jupiter is too high, it denotes arrogance and even if the person is able to achieve great position, he/she may not be able to hold onto it. This is because a balance in personality need always be maintained in life. A long and strong line of head and thumb gives intelligence to handle this Jupiterian energy. Why? Energy can be constructive or destructive – for instance nuclear energy can be harnessed to generate electricity or create nuclear bombs. The potential is huge but mind and intention have to meet.

I have come across hands with a powerful Head Line starting from the Mount of Jupiter but the person is still unable to achieve their professional goals. For one, they have a very high Mount of Jupiter and the first phalange of the thumb is thick like a club (not a desirable personality trait). The possessor of such a thumb is very short tempered and unreasonably obstinate. If challenged, he/she flies into blind rages and ungovernable passions. The person loses all control over themselves and is liable to go to any extreme of violence or crime in such a temper. In fact, the clubbed-shaped thumb (Figure 6.4), has also been designated by the ancient palmistry as 'the murderer's thumb'. The shorter the thumb, the closer the person is to brute passion and lack of self-control. Perseverance is the mother of success. Anger in human beings is destructive.

Research has shown anger has a strong co-relation to career growth. Anger can lead to serious physical and mental health problems as well. So, check this before making any success predictions – even when you see the Line of Head starting from the Mount of Jupiter or power. The possessor of such a thumb should try to make improvements in his/her personality. After all, knowing and understanding oneself and one's temperament – and working on it – can bring amazing changes in life.

Scientific research suggests that on an average, a human being uses only 10% of his/her brain in his/her entire life. The other 90% is working and constitutes our sub-conscious part. The theory I propose is that our destiny is stored in this sub-conscious 90% of our brain, but we are not consciously aware of it. Can we change our destiny code through our *karma* or meditation or may be through hypnosis, when we move deep into the sub-conscious part of the brain? Hypnosis may help identify root problems but ultimately, we have to make constructive changes to our personalities. This is called *karma*. There is nothing in the world that you want and cannot achieve – nobody else has to change – we have to change ourselves. The day we understand this theory, we will be able to achieve success and fulfill our ambitions.

The Mount of Jupiter is a strong indicator of ambition. If there is a star on this mount, sudden success and money comes into life (see encircled portion of Photo 2). I have seen this sign in the hands of those who acquired wealth through their own luck and efforts. A woman possessing such a sign may see herself married to a millionaire. If such a sign is between first and second finger, such persons should be careful in dealing with close relatives and friends.

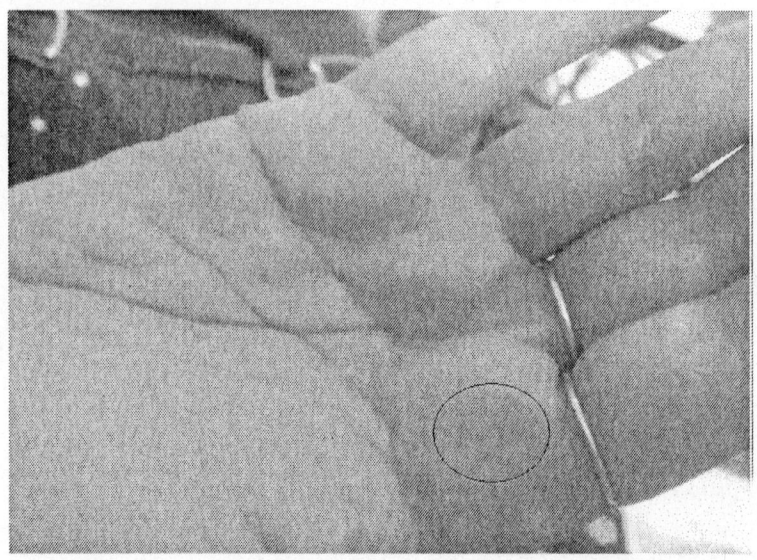

Photo 2: Sign of the Star on Mount of Jupiter (encircled)

The sign of a square on the same mount gives perseverance when success comes. The square sign will also bring obstacles and problems to overcome before achieving success. This sign also conveys spirituality and a philosophical outlook towards life.

The sign of a black dot on the Mount of Jupiter may take a person to great heights, but loss of health and status is also possible. A black dot is a sign of *rahu*, the shadow of the moon. The possessor of such a sign should be careful about his/her health and enemies, even of friends who have access to his/her private secrets. If this dot is near the Life Line, these events occur early in life; if at the top of the mount, then in middle age; and in later years if just below the first finger. Look at Photo 3, of President Barrack Obama holding his lucky charms. There is a black dot on the mount of Jupiter on the left hand, just near the Life Line – this speaks of problems at in the early years of life. Barrack Obama should be careful as this black dot on his Mount of Jupiter may also bring loss of position and status in the future.

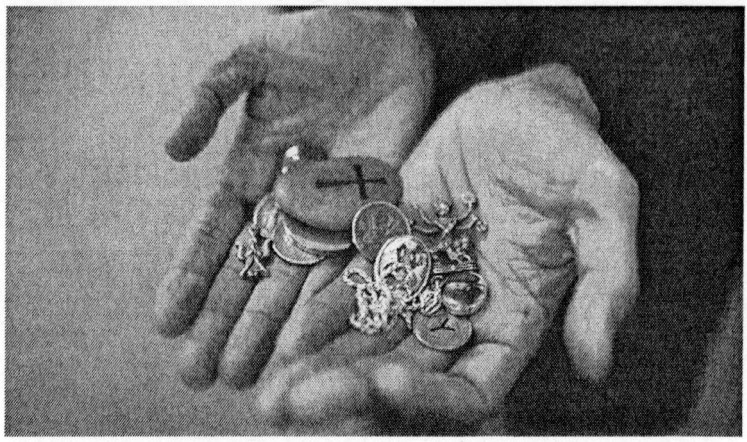

Photo 3: President Obama holding his lucky charms
Source:http://chrismatthewsleg.wordpress.com/2008/06/27/dejected-cms-leg-vows-to-get-me-one-of-those-hindu-monkey-god-charms-like-obama-carries/

One fulfills one's ambitions and professional goals in life, if there is a line coming from the Life Line and ending on the Mount of Jupiter. This ending in a star on the Mount of Jupiter may bring sudden success in life and rise of social status (see Photo 2). If this line ending on the Mount of Jupiter, instead starts from the Mount of Mars near the thumb, then such a person attains high position in the military and armed forces.

A triangle on the Mount of Jupiter, suggests diplomacy, and with a strong thumb, Fate and Head Lines, makes a person into an ambassador, statesman or diplomat. If the Mount of Jupiter, gives ambition, social status and position in society, the Mount of the Sun gives creative talent, fame and prosperity in life.

The sun brings light, warmth, prosperity and growth on earth, similar to the effect of this line in a person's life. I have seen that whenever the Sun becomes strong, there is presence of the Sun Line and even the face of the person glows with inner radiance. But watch out for the glow on the face of the person who comes into the limelight and the whole persona changes. Always look for the shape of the hand along with the strong Mount of the Sun and line. For instance, the presence of the Sun Line on the square hand of a businessman will give him success, whereas in the pointed hand of an artist, it will give fame. Long pointed fingers, a well-developed Mount of the Sun, and a strong Line of the Sun, brings fame through creative talent. Note the pointed shape of the fingers of famous singer Beyonce (see Photo 4).

In a common man's hand, this line would mean improvement in financial position. The Line of the Head is equally important in deciding a career field. A sloping Line of Head (see Beyonce's Line of Head, Photo 4), conveys imagination and creativity. However, the shape of the hand is most important. The Line of Head sloping towards the Mount of the Moon, gives success with publicity. Observe closely the slope of the Head Line in the hands of all the famous people t I have included in Part II of this book – *Destiny Paths of the Rich & Famous*.

Photo 4: Singer Beyonce (pointed shape of fingers)
Source:http://www.iheartthat.com/wp-content/uploads/2006/08 2/ beyonce_nobu.jpg

I would like to include few special Hindu palmistry signs found on the Mount of the Sun (Figure 6.8). In my professional experience, I have observed these signs on the hands of successful and famous people.

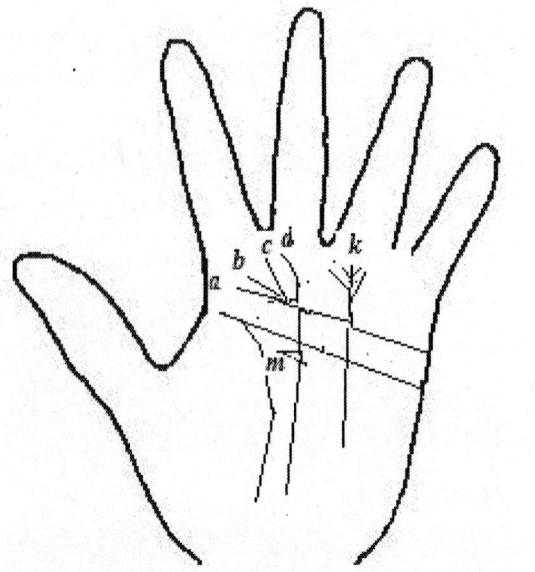

Figure 6.8: Special Hindu signs of fame and success
Abcd = flower; k = seshnaag (serpent;) m = flag

The special sign – abcd, formed by the Fate and Heart Lines, in the shape of the petals of a flower, is considered a sign of wealth, riches and money, though it comes late in life. Another sign – k, is the sign of a special serpent among the Hindus. I have seen this sign on the hand of a famous and most respected personality – this is a very, very rare sign on the hand and leads the person towards liberation of the soul. Yet another sign – m, when found on the Fate or

Sun Lines, brings positive changes in life. This is not a rare sign in palmistry.

Careers in science and its related fields, are seen from the Mount of Mercury. Financial success in business, the stock market and through speculation, is also judged from this mount. A well developed Mount of Mercury suggests eloquence and high intellect. An over-developed Mount of Mercury brings a crafty and clever disposition. Hunger for money may sometime push such a person to cross the line of morals and ethics. An under-developed mount makes the person fickle and lacking in confidence. Diseases of the skin, nerves, digestive system, liver and pancreas, are possible; more so if the Lline of Mercury starts from this mount and ends on the Line of Life. The Line of Mercury is also called the Line of Health in palmistry. The little finger, if long, compensates and removes faults of the mount. With a well developed Mount of Mercury, if inclined towards the Mount of the Sun under the third finger, success in career and money can be predicted.

A well developed Mount of Mercury and Jupiter, gives professional success, money and social status. Such a person generally rises from 32 years of age. It is important to read the signs found on this mount and the little finger, for greater accuracy in predictions. The first phalange of the little finger tells us about the intellectual level, while eloquence and wit are judged from the second phalange. The third phalange shows wisdom about worldly affairs. The length of the little finger and the length of each phalange/segment, add dimension to one's personality. Observe the length of little finger in photos of President Barrack Obama,

Prime Minister Vladmir Putin, Leader of the Congress party, Sonia Gandhi, and the hand print of famous scientist Albert Einstein – they all have a long Finger of Mercury with a good Head Line.

If the Sun Line starts from the Line of Life and ends on the Mount of the Sun below the third finger, the age is marked from the point when it begins from the Life Line. There is growth, opportunities and prosperity and fame, if the hand is artistic. The Sun Line doubly improves fate if this line begins from the Fate Line. When this line begins from the Line of Head, success comes purely through personal effort, hard work and great intellect. The person is a genius if the Head Line bifurcates at the end (see hand print 1 of the great scientist, Albert Einstein – do not miss his Fate Line ending in a sign of the trident – such men are born with a special purpose and are gifts to mankind).

Signs of the trident, star, flag, tree and triangle on the Mount of the Sun, bring success and great name and fame. A strong Line of the Sun, but with negative signs of a dot or island, may bring defamation or bad publicity. Here, fame is through notoriety.

A long Sun Finger adds strength to the mount and the Line of the Sun. However, if the Finger of the Sun is equal in length to the middle/ second finger, it is generally seen in the hands of those who are fond of gambling, taking risks and speculating. Risk-taking ability is huge when the second and third fingers are equal or almost equal in length. A word of caution to such people – always check the signs on your Fate Line and thumb before going in for risky investments.

PALMISTRY The Mystery of Destiny

Knowledge of palmistry can be of immense help to avoid such financial pitfalls.

A long Finger of Mercury gives high intellect, wit and eloquence if the tip of the little finger exceeds the baseline of the first phalange of the third finger(Figure 6.8).

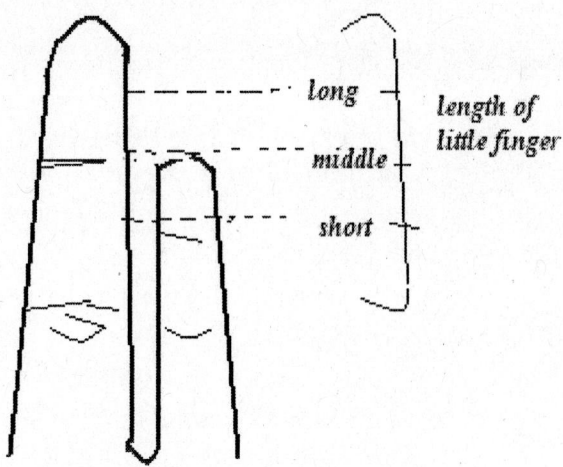

Figure 6.8: Length of the little finger in relation to the third finger

Signs on the Little Finger

1. A plus sign on the first phalange of the little finger gives a broad and robust physique. Mental and physical activities interest these individuals. Sport personalities, including those who play Chess, may have this sign. However, the sign of the cross gives a slim or small but strong physique. Note the difference in these signs (Figure 6.9).

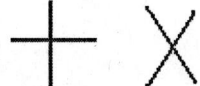

Figure 6.9: sign of plus and cross

2. Vertical line/s on this finger are considered lucky. However, cutting of these vertical lines by thin horizontal line/s, brings hurdles and obstructions in the path of success.

3. Black or red dots on the first phalange of this finger brings wealth. If this dot is in the forepart of this phalange, in addition to money, the person is fond of good food and will gain through real estate deals. Along with other positive signs on the hand, success in book writing is seen. If this dot is right on this phalange, in addition to money, the person is fond of good music and falls in and out of love easily, and moves in the company of powerful men and women.

4. Three straight lines on this finger may bring many awards, position and honour in society. Also gains in landed property, vehicles, and expensive clothes. He/she may travel and visit many foreign lands. In my experience, such persons have an interest in yoga, mystique, philanthropy and spirituality.

5. Two or three straight lines starting from the Mount of Mercury and entering the third phalange of this finger, may mean a career in medicine.

6. Two or three straight lines on the Mount of Mercury and one entering the second phalange, may give money, high social status and professional position.

7. With the sign of a cross on the third phalange of the finger, enmity and jealousy may bring hindrances in the professional path.

8. The sign of a half circle brings wealth through illegal and immoral means.

9. Struggles and hardships, especially in childhood and adolescence, can be predicted if there are many criss-cross lines on the first phalange of this finger.

The Line of the Sun forming an angle with the Line of Mercury, in the shape of a V (mark of Vishnu), brings great luck, money and prosperity. However, if the above lines extend and form the sign of a cross (X), the results are in complete contrast, bringing bad luck, loss and obstacles. The timing/age of such occurrences can be read from the Sun Line and the Life Line.

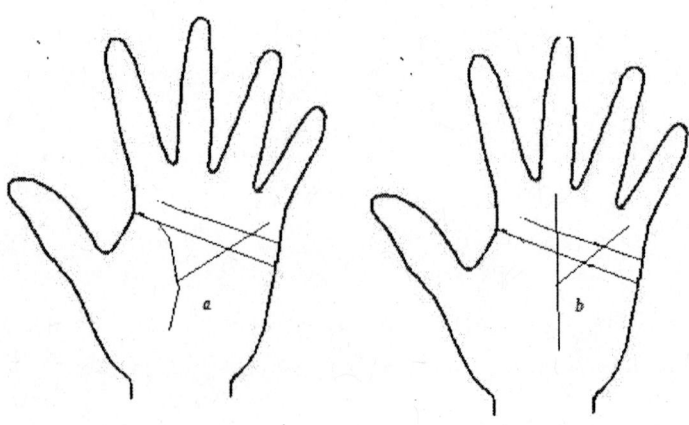

Figure 6.10: Line of mercury
Line a – starting from the Life Line
Line b – starting from the Fate Line

One clear, straight line on the Mount of Mercury shows interest in science and scientific research. Three to five lines on this mount shows a medical profession and more than five lines denotes nursing as a profession or a philanthropist. Medical or soul healers generally have three to five lines on this mount. A branch from the Fate Line running towards this mount, brings success in business. Rich industrialists, bankers and financers have strong Lines of Mercury starting either from the Fate Line or the Line of Life (Figure 6.10/ Lines a & b). However, should the Line of Mercury cross the Line of Life and enter the Mount of Venus, problems of the heart and in matters of the heart/love, bring sorrows and ill health.

The sign of an island, dot, cross or star, on the Line of Mercury may bring financial losses and also loss of health. Next, to read for career and money, is the Mount of the

Moon. A well developed Mount of the Moon gives the possessor creativity and imagination, such as writers, actors, painters and philosophers. Self-centered, suspicious and extremely practical people have an under-developed Mount of the Moon.

An overdeveloped mount makes a person paranoid and extremely sensitive. Saints and spiritual leaders posses a well developed Mount of Jupiter (to guide others), and a line starting from a well developed Mount of the Moon towards the Mount of Mercury. Famous writers, poets and painters posses a line starting from a well developed Mount of the Moon and running towards the Mount of the Sun. World travellers also possess a well developed Mount of Venus – these travel are fruitful and bring money if a line from this mount moves towards the Fate Line, Life Line or the Mount of Venus. The sign of a black dot or island, however, brings stress to one's personal and professional life.

The Lower and Upper Mounts of Mars (Figure 9), gives courage and energy to overcome obstacles and hurdles. Life flows like a river over stones and pebbles, there is excitement, joy and stress. A river is calm when it flows through plains and overflows when angry – likewise, the human soul is a reservoir of energy. How this energy is used decides the flow of life. The one who persists even after setbacks and downfalls, is the winner. The persistence in following one's goals after falling, is the difference between a successful and unsuccessful person. There is no human being who has only happiness and growth in life. Change is the essence of living. It needs courage to begin life anew after failure and loss but if we persist, new seeds germinate and may bear fruits and flowers that are better than before.

Mars on the hand is an indicator of this life energy. Lack of confidence and courage is shown by an under developed mount of Mars. An over developed Mars gives enmity, quarrels and restlessness. The Upper Mount of Mars found below the Mount of Mercury (little finger below the Heart Line and above the Head Line), is well developed in the hands of engineers, mechanics, and those who work in the armed forces or the police. A single vertical line on this mount gives energy to follow one's aims and ambitions even in the face of adversity. Success however, is seen from the Fate and Sun Lines.

However, a single horizontal line running parallel to the Head Line on this mount, cutting the Line of Mercury, may bring health problems, affecting career and profession. Good signs (triangle, trident) or a branch of the Fate Line running towards this mount, brings military honours and position. Negative signs (island, dot, cross, star), on The Upper or Lower Mount of Mars, brings struggle, health and legal problems. A well developed Mount of Venus, however, signifies passion in one's career and the comforts that money can provide. But it is seen more for marriage and relationships. Musicians, actors, painters, artists, designers, beauticians, hairstylists and fields where creative passion is needed, are indicated from this sign but how their careers develop, should be seen from the Fate Line and other mounts.

Part I: VII
TRAVEL

GOD HAS DISPERSED his wonderful creation all over this planet. What little we see or read about this beautiful world excites our imagination to move beyond the limited boundaries of our place of birth. Our minds are inspired to explore the riches of far-away places. Since time immemorial, men have travelled, in search of food, work, and adventure, and possibly in quest of the Self. Travel extends the vision and educates the mind. No wonder that ancient palmistry connected travel with the Mount of the Moon – the mount of imagination and fantasy. Strangely, they also connected the Mount of the Moon with relationships and marriage. Perhaps like travel, love has a strange and magnetic excitement.

Travel written on the hand could be domestic or overseas. Long horizontal lines on the Mount of the Moon indicate travel beyond one's birth place. Also, small lines descending from the Line of Life towards the Mount of the Moon, indicates travel to foreign lands (Figure 7.1).

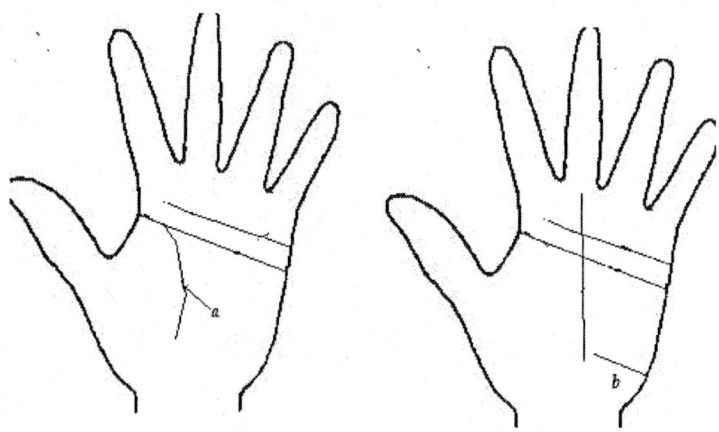

Figure 7.1: Line of Travel
Line a: starting from the Life Line
Line b: horizontal line on Moon

If the Life Line itself divides into two, where one line continues to run towards the mount of Venus and the other towards the Mount of the Moon, the person not only travels, but migrates to a foreign land. If the line running towards the Mount of the Moon is stronger, it promises permanent foreign settlement. If both the lines are of equal strength, the person is not a settler but a traveller. Such a person travels all his life.

If, the Life Line, instead of running round the Mount of Venus, leaves its usual place and goes towards the Mount of the Moon, the person migrates and breathes his last on foreign soil (Figure 7.2).

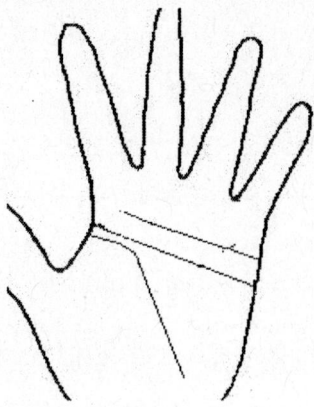

Figure 7.2: Permanent settlement in a foreign land

At the age indicated by a branch line leaving the main Life Line, Fate Line or Sun Line, along with good signs of palmistry (triangle, rising line), travel brings prosperity. However, if the Sun or Fate Line, suddenly ends, breaks or has the sign of an island, travel to a foreign country may not prove to be prosperous. The Sun Line and Fate Line should always be seen for prosperity if the person is travelling for work or planning to migrate. If, there is a sign of the cross or star on the travel line, there could be some danger in the travel. Professionally, I feel such a star or cross appears on the Travel Line very close to the date of travel, say a month or so before. Danger to life is also possible if the Life Line also has such a sign.

Today, there are many water sports and many people undertake water adventures for fun and excitement. The sign of a star or cross on the Mount of the Moon but not on any horizontal line, could also mean danger from such water adventures. This sign, not touching the Line of Travel, means danger from drowning or some accident in water but not necessarily while travelling.

Again, today air travel is the most used and fastest means of travel across the world, so a star or cross sign on the Travel Line, need not mean danger associated only with water travel, as given in ancient palmistry books. The Mount of the Moon signifies all such travels where the person crosses the boundaries of one's birth place. In olden days, travel through water was the most popular means of transportation, unlike today, hence the prediction of death through drowning. I would say that a star or cross on the Travel Line means danger even for air travel. The sign of the square, around the star or cross, means escape from danger (Figure 7.3).

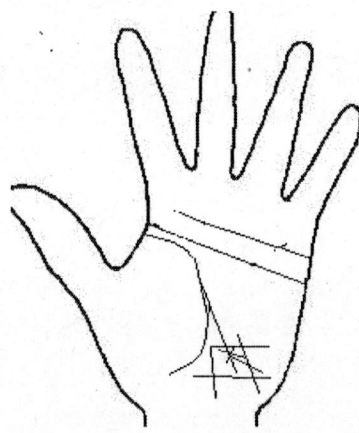

Figure 7.3: Escape from danger on a journey

It is also unlucky, to have Travel Lines turning down towards the wrist. This indicates a journey undertaken for work but with no fruitful results, and only expenditure.

Due to modern technical advancements in communications and travel, the world is shrinking. More and more people are travelling to foreign lands. These Travel Lines have more significance now than ever before. But with economic globalization and uncertainties looming large, it may be a good idea to use knowledge of palmistry before undertaking a journey. Any knowledge that can make our present life easy and less stressful is worth exploring!

PART I: VIII
CHILDREN

GOD CREATED THIS universe so that it could reproduce its own kind. Furthermore, in his creation, man was placed above plants and animals, perhaps the last stage of evolution before reaching HIM. He added emotions in human beings so we could experience love, anger, mercy, forgiveness, cruelty, happiness and sorrow. The journey of life is not easy for anyone. It is not His intention to make us suffer but for us to understand life and so become better human beings. Tough times rather than good times, teach us to be more humble and humane. God is not a dictator whose laws and rules we all have to follow or we are punished. Instead, he lets us create our own destiny plan.

Each soul creates his own destiny through his own *karma*. Our *karma* follows us in our life journey in the form of sorrow or happiness. The ancient Hindu scriptures reveal that in order to experience a state of complete happiness, all negative emotions such as anger, jealousy and ego, have to be removed, only then can we experience a state of complete happiness. A soul has to evolve to reach Him. This is not an easy task, only a very few souls like the

Buddha, are able to evolve to that level. But all human beings learn through difficult lessons. Inmy experience, power, money and fame teach less. Hardships, sorrow and miseries are all self-inflicted. This cycle of birth and death continues till a soul eliminates all negative emotions. This is the evolution of the soul. For continuation of life, God's plans gets even bigger.

The ability to procreate beings like oneself, and with joy, is God's amazing plan. Because science is dedicated to facts and details, often the big picture is lost. Man has created science but science, till today, has not been able to create Man. The only breakthrough recently is creation of the 'synthetic cell', and in fact, wrong media hype calling it the creation of 'synthetic life'. What the team of scientists led by Craig Venter, has done, does not amount to creating new life from scratch. No science can ever duplicate God's work. In procreation, God has added the spice of 'love'. All human beings love their children from the moment they are conceived. All parents have unconditional love for their children, and this is God's *maya* (illusion).

Strange as it may sound, the ancient Hindu scriptures write that when there is attachment towards anything or anyone; it is the beginning of suffering. All bonds, even bonds of love, bring pain and suffering in life.

The bond of marriage in order to procreate, became a social and moral foundation – but not necessarily now in the presently emerging world. So, I have made a slight correction to ancient palmistry and present below my own knowledge and experience in palmistry vis-à-vis children.

The lines that indicate children are upright lines M on the Relationship Line, and A and B on the Mount of Mercury (Figure 8.1). Lines A and B are Relationship Lines. Line B is the darker line of the two and is the Line of Marriage. Vertical lines on this line imply children through marriage, whereas vertical lines on line A imply children out of wedlock. If the Relationship Line A is light and short in length, children are indicated through physical union but no relationship forms between the couple.

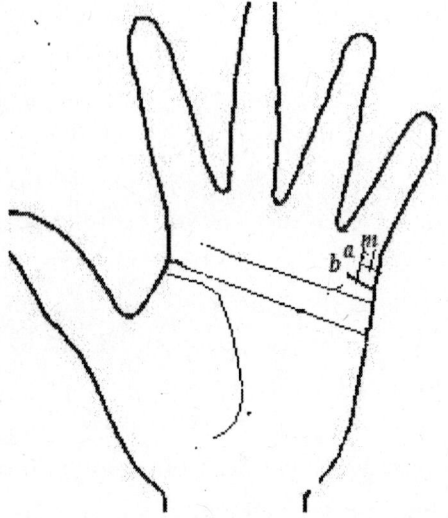

Figure 8.1: The Line of Children

Children lines on the Mount of Mercury are very fine and not easily visible. To see them, press the Line of Marriage with the thumb and then release the pressure. Better still, use a magnifying hand lens.

If vertical lines M of children, reach the Heart Line, he/she will be very affectionate and caring as a parent. Sometimes, for such a parent, children may mean even more than his/her partner. According to ancient palmistry, thick lines signify boys and thin lines girls. Personally, I feel this needs more investigation and research. I am not able to verify this ancient belief. To me, it seems that with the changing times, the difference in the gender role has decreased in both the social and economic worlds due to greater participation of women in spheres and roles normally perceived to be only for men in ancient times. Women and men both now carry forward family names and inheritance. Also, unlike olden times, both follow similar roles in taking care of their elderly parents. Deep and long lines on the palm imply greater impact, role and emotional care.

If line M is near the edge of the pal (Figure 8.1), the child is born early in the relationship. The age of bearing children can be read as the line moves from the edge towards the palm.

Health of children can be predicted by the strength of this line as well. Negative signs (star, island, cross, break), on the vertical line of children, affect the health and longevity of the child. A star and a black dot on the Line of Children are not considered favourable signs for longevity (Figure 8.2).

The mount of Venus, also has markings for children (Fgure 8.3). Vertical lines on this mount towards the thumb are lines of children.

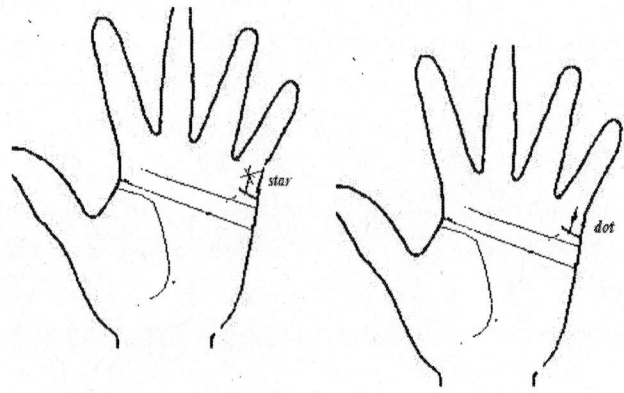

Figure 8.2: Signs on Line of Children

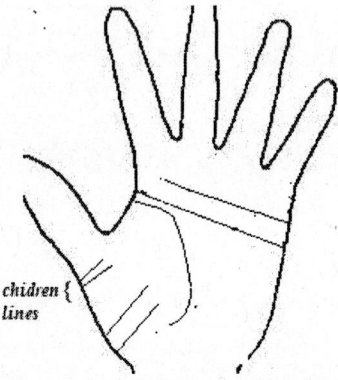

Figure 8.3: The Line of Children

Count the number of lines on this mount for the number of children the person will have. Note the lines for children are towards the thumb and not the wrist (Figure 8.3).

Medical problems, if any, for the mother during pregnancy and childbirth, can also be read from a woman's hand. Bracelets on the wrist are good indicators for the overall health of a person. The top bracelet, if curved and rising in form of an arch towards the palm, indicates difficulty during childbirth (Figure 8.4).

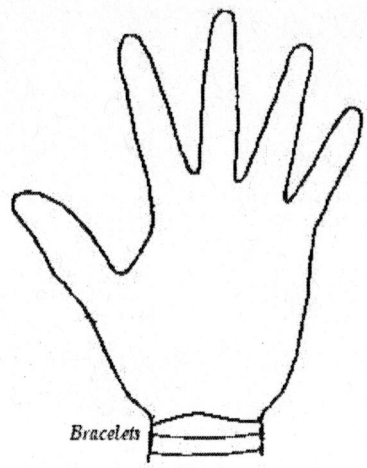

Figure 8.4: Bracelets indicating the health of the mother

If all three bracelets are arched, there may be danger to the life of the woman during her pregnancy or during childbirth. The Life Line should also be studied carefully before making any predictions. The fertility of a woman can also be seen from the palm. If the Health Line intersects the Head Line in a star, the woman may have difficulty in conceiving naturally (Figure 8.5).

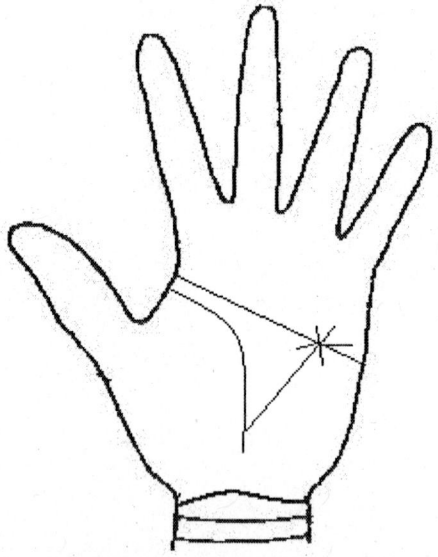

Figure 8.5: Star indicating infertility

The role of modern women has changed dramatically. Statistical research indicates women today delay child-bearing and this has an effect on fertility. Advanced treatments such as IVF (in vitro fertilization), do help to overcome the age related decline in fertility, however, there is now an unrealistic expectation that medical science can undo the effects of ageing. Women who have broad (not high) and well-developed Mounts of Venus, three straight lines of bracelets, line M of children on the Relationship Line and vertical lines on the Mount of Venus towards the thumb, have high fertility and hence the probability of bearing children is also high.

PART I: IX
SPIRITUALITY

SCIENCE AND SPIRITUALITY, the two diametrically opposite points of the same line segment called Life. One deals with facts and the other with beliefs, yet the two are connected. This connection is Life and its relation to he Universe. Life has the essence, the spirit or *atma*. Once this spirit or *atma* leaves the physical being, what is left behind merges with the Universe, *ashes to ashes*.

Ancient Hindu scriptures say the spirit or *atma* never dies, like energy, it changes form. If we cannot understand how the spirit or *atma* exists, we should consider the limited powers of our minds, and in this universe there is so much more that we cannot understand. The spirit or *atma* may exist inside all living beings, though we cannot tell how – we ought to perhaps consider by what inexplicable evidence its existence is supported. I have said this much and I leave it to my readers' discretion to investigate further. My beliefs are mine alone cannot be superimposed. I have studied both science and occult sciences, and support both – because it is the connection called 'life' I am interested in.

Hindus believe in rebirth or reincarnation. They think that only the physical body dies but the spirit or the soul inside the body, does not. After the death of the physical body, the soul or *atma*, comes back to earth in a newborn body. This transmigration of the soul to a new body, is influenced by past *karmas*. Where will the soul take birth? Who will be his/her new parents and family? Why is a person born in a palace as a prince while another is born as a pauper on the street? We neither know nor have control over this advantage or disadvantage. It can be called the *karma* genetics of the soul.

Life is a battleground of constant struggles. No period, good or bad, remains forever. We all are born with a certain destiny, and it is our personality, our will power, our intelligence and our present *karmas* that shape our 'journey of life' on this earth. What is *karma*? It means 'action' or 'act'. Each person follows a destiny path, set by the person's own past and present acts or *karma*. Not God, but we create our destiny, through our *karma*. God has created this as the 'Law of the Universe' and made us Captains of this Law. Like the law of conservation of energy, our *karma* can neither be created nor destroyed. but it changes form, and this form can be happiness, wealth, disease or sorrows It is for a person to understand this and make improvements in his/her *karma*.

The Hindus believe that the soul travels through many life journeys. Between birth and death, in one life journey, it may acquire many treasures and lands but after death, leaves behind all these worldly treasures and carries only its *karma* to the next birth. There may be many who may not believe this theory of reincarnation, but all worldly pursuits end with life, this much. Even a non-believer agrees with. What is important is how happy and blissful this journey of life is. If God is impartial, then why do the windfalls of luck and wheels of fortune favour only a few? The Hindu ideology or Law of *Karma*, may possibly be the answer. This Law of *Karma* is based on Newton's Law of Cause and Effect – for every action there is a reaction. This chain of *karmic* retribution can only be broken when you are willing to pay your *karmic* debt willingly, without resentment, selfishness or bitterness in your heart.

As our soul travels through different lives, it carries its balance *karma* (positive-negative balance). If the balance is in the negative, the journey of the soul has more challenges, and if the balance is positive, there is greater abundance and such a person is sometimes called 'lucky' or 'destiny's child'.

Destiny is strange, it brings 'forgetfulness' – *karmic* amnesia. The mind has three levels – the conscious, sub-conscious and un-conscious (Sigmund Freud's theory). All the fruits and all the testing cross-roads of life, are stored in some little corner of our un-conscious brain. The brain transmits this information through nerves to the hands. The lines on the palm are the blueprint of this destiny.

What is 'good' *karma*? We do not have to search for the answer, our own conscience can tell us what is good/bad and right/wrong. We just have to listen to that little voice that comes from the mind. When we do something opposite to what our 'voice' tells us, no matter how we try to find justifications for the same, the Universal Law of *Karma* becomes operative and there is retribution.

The Law of Conservation of Energy says that energy is never lost but changes form. For instance, heat energy changes to light. Similarly, the spirit or *atma*, changes one body for another after the first existence ends. This changing of form continues till the energy of *atma* reaches its pure form. The purification of the spirit may take many life journeys from birth to death to evolve into a pure form. When one human being relates to another with understanding on a spiritual level, there is evolution of the soul. Evolution of the soul is a continuous process and full of difficulties and challenges. There are two worlds – the physical and the deluding world of *maya*. *Maya* is the power that blinds, binds and deludes us, and we forget the real purpose of our lives. Through the deluding power of *maya*, the material world becomes our purpose, and in pursuit of our wrong aims, we cheat, lie, hate, feel jealous, and even kill, and carry *karmic* debt into the next birth.

Sunlight causes cloud formation through the evaporation process and the clouds thus formed cover the sun and block sunlight. This is possibly the most interesting and beautiful phenomena in nature to explain *maya* or delusion. God created human beings and *maya* in human beings stops us from reaching God. But, when there is the bright sunlight of knowledge in human beings, it scatters the cloud of *maya*/delusion, and breaks the bondages of sorrow and misery. We all are moving towards our own end, though it is a very gradual process, so why not make this precious life worthwhile for ourselves and for others? Everything in this universe is changing but we cannot feel this change – why? Because of our ignorance. Why are material goals only important in life and if they are, then why do they not give us complete happiness? Again, because of ignorance. We have forgotten the need to connect to our soul (spirit) for happiness and contentment. When we are not happy and contented souls, we make the lives of others miserable as well. This is like a nuclear chain reaction – once this nuclear bomb of unhappiness gets activated, it carries with it the potential to destroy the entire world.

Where does palmistry come into this? We are all motivated by our *karmic* destiny to follow a set path, and knowledge of palmistry helps read this path. Once we realize that there is, some law working over and above us, we may try to be better human or spirit beings. People and situations exist because we have created them. Think of the world we live in – full of hatred, violence, jealousy, terrorism, disease – and think of *maya*/delusion, which leads us to it. Think of one's own personal destiny path and personal spirit improvement. The strength of our own spirit makes our own individual world beautiful. This collective individual spiritual improvement can make this world a better place.

PART I: X
ILLNESS & DISEASE

IN WESTERN PALMISTRY, lifespan is judged from the Line of Life, but in ancient Hindu palmistry, lifespan is judged from the Line of the Heart. Other than the Life Line, we have five principal lines on the hand—Heart, Head, Fate, Health, Sun/Fortune. The Fate and Sun Lines are connected to professional growth, prosperity, fame and reputation. So they do not directly affect longevity.

The Head Line indicates the intellect of an individual and also the working of the brain. If the brain stops functioning, for instance in cases of brain damage, life is still possible though the person may be in a state of coma. However, according to medical experts, the mind or brain-related diseases can cause heart failure or other diseases. Mind or brain-related diseases are possible if there are negative signs (dot, break, bar, island, star) on the Head Line. In addition, if the colour of the palm is dark red, high blood pressure is possible. As per medical experts, if one has high blood pressure or hypertension, the heart has to work harder to pump blood. This pressure can strain the heart, damage blood vessels, and increase the risk of heart attack. Also, diseases of the mind like depression, increase the risk of heart disease. So, if there are negative signs (dot, break, bar, island, star) on both the Head and Heart lines, grave danger can be perceived to the life of that individual.

In palmistry, great danger to life can also be perceived if there are negative signs (dot, break, bar, island, star), on both the Heart and Health Lines. The latter tells us about the functioning of the liver and digestive system. Scientific studies have shown the rate of heart failure increases in concordance with diabetes, hypertension, high blood pressure, diet and lifestyle habits. People with diabetes also tend to develop heart disease or have strokes at an earlier age than other people. Diabetes have at least twice the risk of heart failure as other people.

So we can say, directly or indirectly, that negative signs (dot, break, bar, island, star), on both the Health and Heart Line/ Head and Heart Lines, affect longevity. But most importantly, unlike in ancient times, with the amazing medical advances of today, most heart diseases are curable. In my experience, danger to life can also be predicted from the heart if there is a break or the sign of a star on the Heart Line or similar signs either on the Head or Health Line. Since the Line of Life is an overall barometer of life, re-confirmation of this from the Line of Life should also be done.

Contemporary medical technology and clinical expertise are most successful in diagnosis, treatment and prevention of illness and diseases. Medical palmistry does not fall into the realm of conventional medicine but can be grouped under complementary and alternative medicine. The beauty of medical palmistry lies in predicting the timing of the disease, diagnosis, severity and finally the outcome of medical treatment. By reading the signs on the palm, diseases and illnesses can be predicted far in advance, even before the onset of the actual disease. For instance, negative signs (star, break, and dot) on the Heart Line indicate ailments of the heart in palmistry and this can be predicted much before the actual onset of the disease. This should not surprise science; after all, science calls this (in its own language), congenital or genetic disorder. Medical advancement is still undergoing genetic research. Would it not help mankind if medical science borrows the knowledge of medical palmistry for treatment of illnesses and disease?

In ancient palmistry, the Health Line was also linked to success in business and one's profession. Statistical research also shows co-relation between health and career. Health should never be overlooked in worldly pursuits. Like one's bank balance, our health also increases our net worth. We tend to undervalue health and overvalue wealth. Worries and mental stress are the main reasons for ill-health. Break the word 'disease' into 'dis-ease', which means our soul is not at ease and is holding onto physical or emotional issues. For our own good we should let all negativity go and only then can we move forward in life. The *Bhagvad Gita*, the holy book of the Hindus, says we all come into this world empty handed and will also go out of it empty handed – all that we acquire between birth and death will all be left behind, so what is not yours should not grieved for. Be ambitious, follow your dreams, and give your best shot to fulfill your hopes and dreams, but stay detached towards the outcome or results. This may be tough to follow, but if we can, life becomes easier and happier. The Almighty has written our destiny in our hands to read the scheme of things and move forward with better understanding. That is not to say, money or acquisition of material comfort are bad, but attachment towards them can bring sorrow and misery. Life is simply to enjoy what is given.

From my own professional experience and knowledge of palmistry, I am outlining a few illnesses and diseases that can be diagnosed through palmistry. The shape of the hand, the texture of the skin, nails and colour, are the first things to look for.

Nails are made of a tough protein called keratin, and besides protecting the fingers, indicate one's health condition. Long pink nails indicate intelligence and good health. If the fingers and nails are short, the possessor is likely to suffer from dental troubles. White spots on the nails give warning of weak nerves in advance. Deep horizontal lines on the nails show mental trauma. White semi-circle moons at the base of the nails, especially the thumb, are signs of good health.

A broad hand with smooth texture and well-developed mounts or pads, and slight pink colouring of the palm, are signs of good health. Any deviations from this indicates the possibility of disease and needs to be further investigated.

High Blood Pressure / Hypertension

If the colour of the palm is not pink but unusually dark red or there are red spots on the palm, and is warm to the touch, diseases of the blood such as blood pressure and hypertension is a possibility. The sign of a black dot on the Head Line indicates migraine or severe headaches, whereas a red dot on the Head Line indicates complications caused by high blood pressure. A Head Line which is short in length with a break or has the sign of a star, indicates extreme tension affecting the functioning of the brain (Figure 10.1).

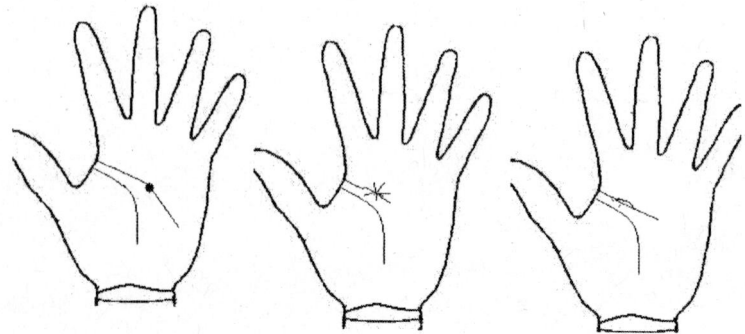

Figure 10.1: Stress and anxiety causing blood pressure

Many statistical studies have shown anxiety and stress are linked to temporary increases in blood pressure, but not to chronic high blood pressure. Stress and tensions are cumulative factors causing high blood pressure. The probability of having chronic blood pressure increases when, in addition to the above mentioned signs, the Mount of Mars near the thumb is over-developed, the palm has a red colour and the top phalange of the thumb is fleshy. If the semi-circle moon on all five fingernails is missing, the circulation of blood is poor and this increases the possibility of high blood pressure after the age of 40 years. Medium or small moons at the base of all nails indicate normal blood pressure.

Jaundice

The colour of the nails and palm tends to be is yellow in cases of jaundice. When the moon-like semi-circles on the nails and colour of the nails is slightly blue, this indicates jaundice. The growth of the index fingernail almost stops. The Line of Health rising from the Mount of Mercury under the little finger, is wavy and moves downwards towards the Life Line. A dark brown (sometimes blue) spot, can be seen on the Line of Life. In my professional experience, this spot appears during or after the occurrence of the disease (Figure 10.2).

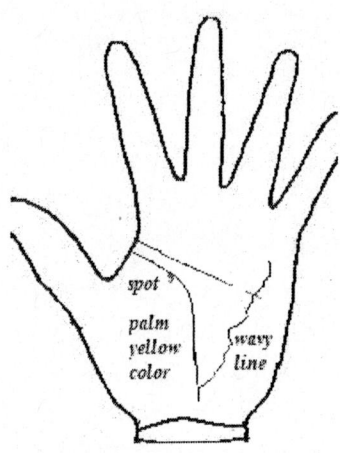

Figure 10.2: Signs of Jaundice

Arthritis

Vitamin D is a fat soluble vitamin that is necessary for healthy bones. It is essential for a range of metabolic processes, and almost all Vitamin D comes from sunlight. A very small amount of Vitamin D comes from the diet.

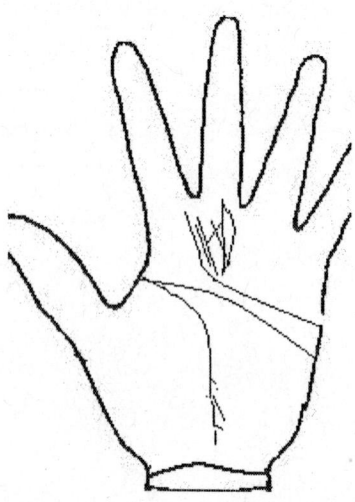

Figure 10.2: Signs for Arthritis

Negative signs on the Mount of the Sun or an underdeveloped Mount of the Sun indicates problems with the bones. In addition, the nails are generally broad and longitudinal ridges on the nails, splitting at the ends, can be seen. There are also the signs of a grill or star on the Mount of Saturn, and sometimes minute dots on the edges of the palm lines (Figure 10.3). The Mounts of the Sun and Saturn are displaced towards each other (maybe together). The Mount of Mars near the thumb, is also raised.

Asthma

The first sign to look for relating to asthma is the quadrangle, formed by the Head and Heart Lines. If the Head and Heart Lines are very close to each other, forming a narrow quadrangle, this indicates the possibility of asthma. If there is an island formation on the Mount of Jupiter, this indicates diseases of the respiratory organ or wheezing. In addition, the presence of a spot, cross or island under the Mount of Saturn, and a black spot in a narrow quadrangle, increases the probability of asthma, (Figure 10.2).

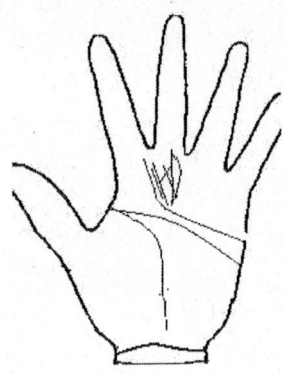

Figure 10.2: Signs for Asthma

Also, the Health Line will not be well-formed. For any serious health problem, the Life Line will have descending lines. A line from inside the Mount of Venus, cutting the lines of Life and Head and ending in a star or grille on the Upper Mount of Mars, also indicates asthma.

Heart Diseases

Congenital heart defects are problems with the heart's structure that are present at birth. These defects change the normal flow of blood through the heart. The first sign to look for this is in the nails. The nails will be short and mostly square in shape. Semi-moon-like circles may be completely missing or there may be very large moons – this is an indication of imperfect blood circulation. A high level of blood cholesterol is possible if hands are cold, with coarse, puffy skin and a thick, defective Heart Line. The Heart Line made up of several small lines, indicates weak heart muscles. Fine perpendicular lines on the Mount of Saturn, touching the Heart Line, indicate defects in heart functioning.

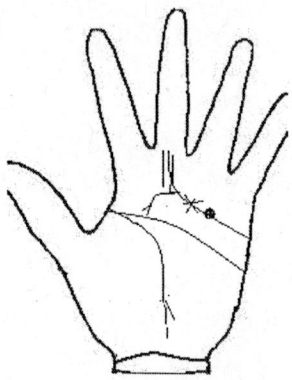

Figure 10.2: Signs of heart disease

In my professional experience I have always found that negative signs (break, bar, black dot, star) are sure signs of heart disease, especially if the Heart Line becomes weak after these signs (Figure 10.2). Any descending branch line from the Heart Line under the Mount of Saturn, indicates medical intervention, probably surgery (Figure 10.2). For any serious health problems, the Life Line will always have descending lines

Please note that some of the diseases that I have mentioned, have been verified by me in my professional experience. Other diseases mentioned in ancient palmistry but for which I have not got satisfactory results, I have not included them here.

Part II
DESTINY PATHS
OF THE RICH & FAMOUS

Included in this section are palm-photos of some rich and famous people. I respect the privacy of celebrities and hold the opinion that it would be incorrect to intrude into their private lives. Hence, I am including only the personality and career analysis, purely for the benefit of the study of palmistry, and for those who believe in destiny. It is my intention to help people appreciate the value of palmistry through the hand analysis of these celebrities. Many of us have unrealistic expectations from ourselves or feel depressed during hard times. Once we learn to read our own personal destiny in our hands, it may change our perceptions and we can be more open and positive in life.

Today, we live in a world over-run by poverty, greed, crime and violence. Changes in individual perception and attitude are important and can alter social psychology globally. As with any field of study, palmistry has its critics but they too, have a role in its progress. Any study that can help mankind in any way, is certainly worth exploring.

Hand of Barrack Obama ~ President, United States of America

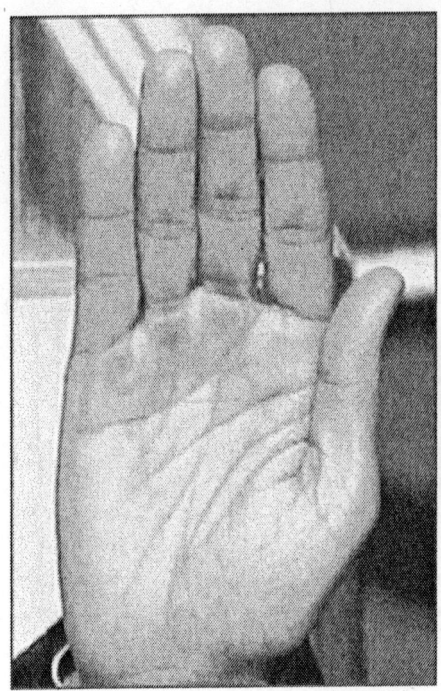

Photo 7: Hand of President Obama
Source: http://handfacts.wordpress.com/category/hand-reading/page/3/

The shape of the hand and the long thumb, indicate the intense, driving power within and a strong will power to pursue one's goals in life. The thumb should always be seen first in personality analysis. Barrack Obama has a long thumb. The tip of his thumb exceeds the base of the first finger. The stronger the personality of the person, the greater his chance to succeed in life. The second phalange of the thumb is longer than the first and slightly waist-like in shape – this indicates a logical and legal bent of mind. President Obama is a graduate of Harvard Law School.

The Wheat Line or *Pushpa Rekha*, as described in chapter 2, is in shape of an eye. If the Wheat Line is shapes like an eye, the possessor is considered lucky and prospers in life.

Look at Photo 7, the little finger is exceptionally long. A long little finger denotes a position of power in government or the judiciary. This finger also suggests intellect and writing and communication skills. Barrack Obama, on the basis of his grades and a writing competition, was selected Editor of the **Harvard Law Review**, a journal of legal scholarship. He has showcased his writing skills in his published books. A long little finger also gives success in writing. His book, *The Audacity of Hope*, became number one on both the *New York Times* and Amazon.com bestsellers lists.

When all the lines on the palm are extremely clear, such a person says and does things as he feels and is not a superficial personality. There is always the desire to work for the people. It is reported that Obama put law school and corporate life on hold after college, and moved to Chicago, where he became a community organizer with a cause – to improve living conditions in poor neighborhoods plagued with crime and high unemployment.

The insides of all the fingers and thumb are softly padded – such a person is fond of music. The long thumb and well-developed Mount of Jupiter below the first finger, shows the inclination towards politics. Obama began his political career as an Illinois state senator. He began his run for the presidency after a close campaign against Hillary Rodham Clinton, in the Democratic Party presidential primaries. Obama's eloquence and communication skills, in addition to all his other qualities, won him the party's nomination. In this example and examples of other world leaders, you will notice the significance of the long thumb, long little finger, Mount of Jupiter and Line of Head.

The most remarkable feature, for those interested in palmistry, is Barrack Obama's Head Line. He has a long sloping Head Line starting below the Mount of Jupiter (see Photo 7). There is a wide gap between the Head Line and the Life Line at the start. The Mount of Jupiter gives social status and suggests a political career and is also a seat of power in palmistry. There may be many interested in pursuing a political career but only a few chosen ones achieve success. The long Line of Head, starting from the Mount of Jupiter, the long thumb and little finger, bring success in politics, and is found on the hands of most world leaders. A line rising from the Life Line and reaching the mount of power – Jupiter, and a long Line of Head, also rising from this mount, gives amazing political success (see Photo 7 & Illustration 7). This indicates intellect and luck supports success in one's endeavours.

Another interesting feature is the double Line of Life. Readers will see this line commonly on the hands of most world leaders. Look at the semi-circle around the thumb (see Photo 7 & Illustration 7). There is a sister line running parallel to the Life Line. This line is a gift from God, carrying positive *karma* from previous births. This line also protects Obama from all dangers and gives strong health. This double Line of Life makes the person conscious of his health and physical fitness and it is widely reported that Barrack Obama is extremely fitness conscious.

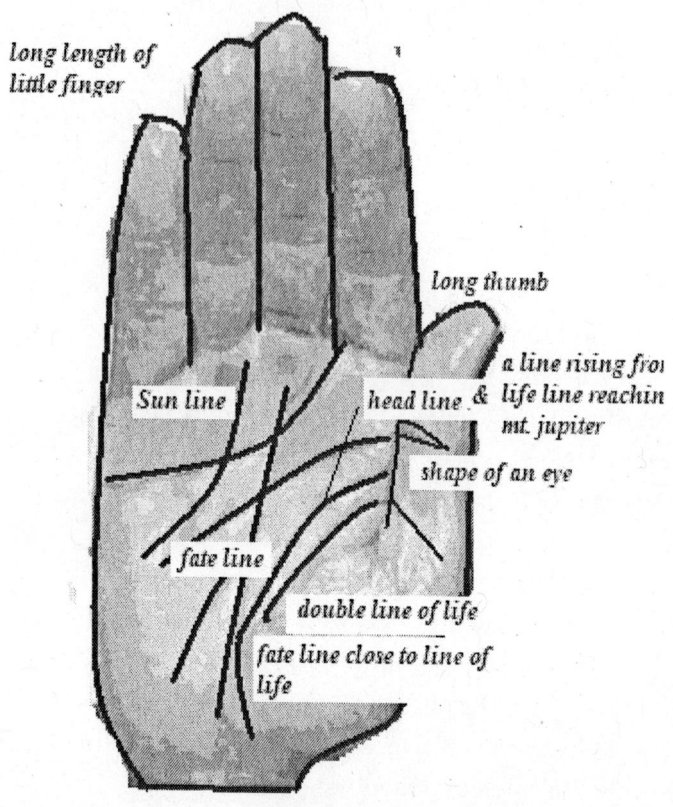

Illustration 7: Hand sketch of President Obama

Obama has two Fate Lines – one starting near the Line of Life and the other starting from the Mount of the

Moon. The difficulties he faced and influence of family in the early years of life, can be seen from the Fate Line lying close to the Line of Life. Creating his own destiny purely through personal efforts, is indicated from the second Fate Line, starting from the Mount of the Moon. Barack Obama was raised by a single mother and his grandparents. His family was not wealthy.

The double Fate Line, double Line of Life, long thumb, long little finger, and a Head Line starting from the mount of power, are the most significant indications on the palm of President Obama. Such a person is truly 'chosen' by destiny. However, the black spot on his left hand on the seat of power, the Mount of Jupiter, can bring loss of position and status (see Photo 3). This is not a favourable sign. This spot will bring him to the seat of power first – and then may result in a sudden loss of position.

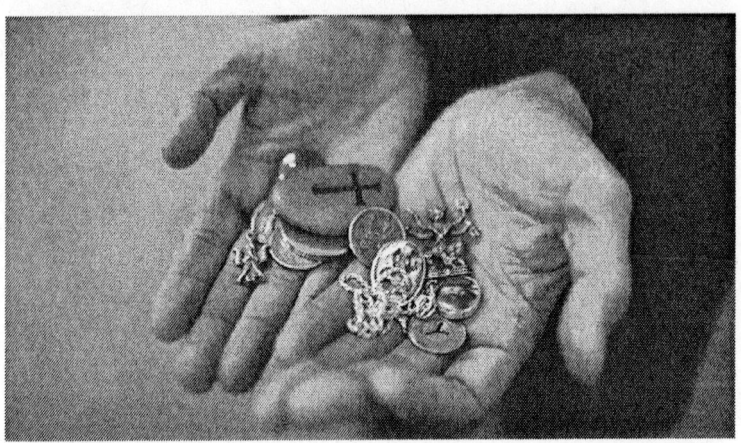

Photo 3: The black spot on President Obama's left palm
Source:http://chrismatthewsleg.wordpress.com/2008/06/27/dejected-cms-leg-vows-to-get-me-one-of-those-hindu-monkey-god-charms-like-obama-carries/

PALMISTRY The Mystery of Destiny

Hand of Vladmir Putin ~ Prime Minister of Russia

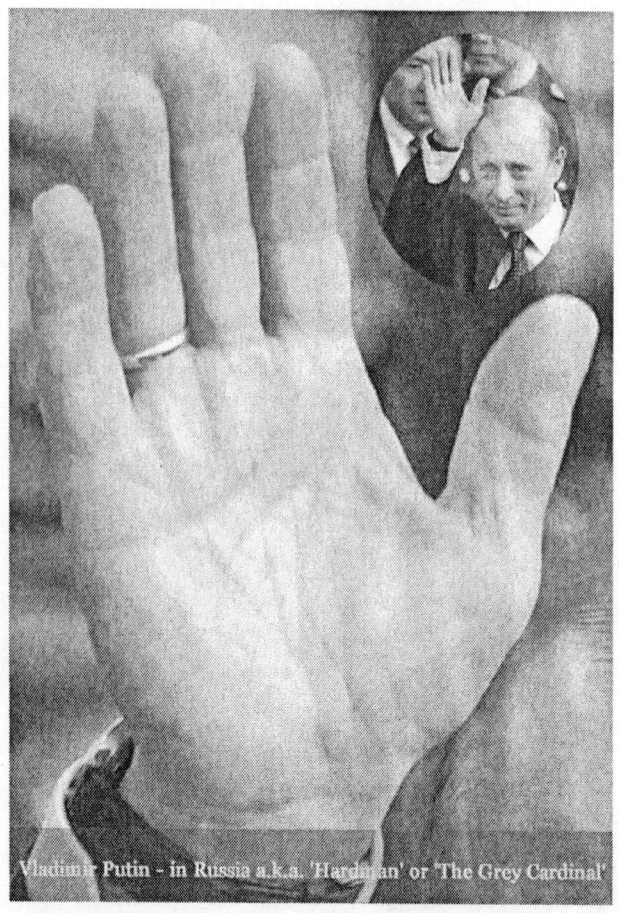

Photo 8: Hand of Vladmir Putin
Source: *http://handfacts.wordpress.com/category/hand-reading/*

The first thing to notice in palmistry is the shape of the hand and the thumb. Note the shape of the hand of Russian

Prime Minister, Vladmir Putin. The shape of the palm is broad at the base and thick; the fingers are shorter in relation to the length of the palm. The fingers are square shaped and thick. This is the hand of a man ruled by the planet Mars – the planet of physical and mental energy. In such a person, physical sports and exercise will always be of interest. From the sixth grade, Putin took great interest in sambo and judo. According to media reports, Prime Minister Putin is probably the first world leader to not only learn and practice judo, but to also move into the advanced levels of the sport. It is reported that Putin, on a state visit to Japan, was invited to show the students and Japanese officials different judo techniques.

The most significant marking on his palm is double the Line of Lfe. One Line of Life begins with the Line of Head (see Photo 8 & Illustration 8). This indicates the humble early years of his life. Putin's book, *Ot Pervogo Litsa* (*In the First Person*), speaks of his humble beginnings. The starting point of the second Line of Life is really amazing as it begins from the Mount of Jupiter or the mount of power (see Photo 8 & Illustration 8). This is a very interesting reading as it suggests a change in life, a complete contrast to his early life.

The other amazing and interesting feature in palmistry, is the number of Fate Lines. There are three – one starting from the Life Line; one within the Life Line from the Mount of Venus; and the third starting from the wrist. All the Fate Lines have different starting points, but they all turn at the end, towards the Mount of Jupiter, the seat of power. It is uncommon to have such amazing Fate Lines.

They pave the path of destiny – such a man may have the most humble beginnings but will reach the most powerful seat of power in his country.

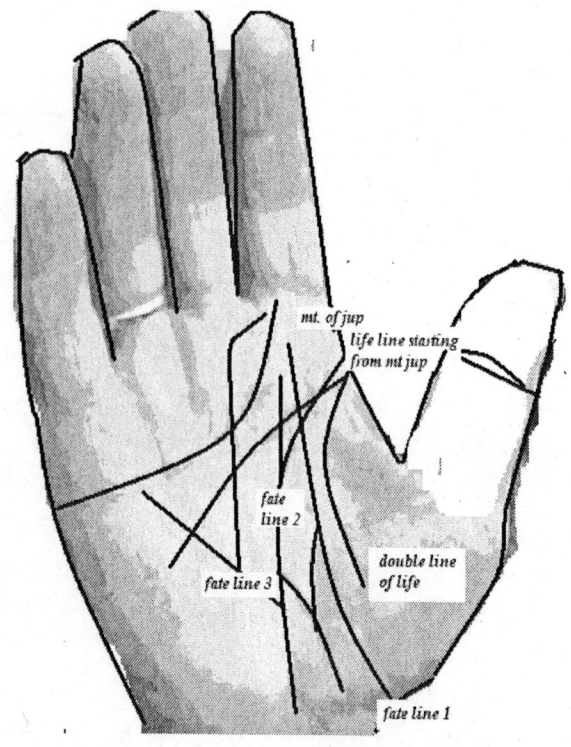

Illustration 8: Hand of Vladmir Putin

In example 1 of President Obama, and in this example, notice how significant the Mount of Jupiter is. Now, on Putin's thumb, the broad face with the pad at the center of the thumb, shows extreme intelligence and will power to sustain and face all kinds of situations in life. The tip of the little finger reaches above the base line of the third finger –

this again shows a powerful position in government and good communication skills. Again we see the similarity of the long length of little finger in example 1 and example 2 – almost all world leaders are gifted with oratory and communication skills. Like President Obama, Putin is also a law graduate and has a double Line of Life. This indicates humble beginnings and a rise to the seat of power, plus protection from all dangers and enemies.

Putin's rise to Russia's highest office is both amazing and interesting. Three Fate Lines (see Illustration 8), all turn and end on the Mount of Jupiter. Especially note the turning of Fate Line 3 towards the Mount of Jupiter. Putin was first inaugurated as Russia's President in the year 2000. In the year 2004, he was re-elected as President of Russia. In the year 2008, he was appointed as the Prime Minister of Russia. Fate Line 1 (see Illustration 8), starting inside the Life Line, from the Mount of Venus and reaching Mount of Jupiter, connects the planet Venus of love, money and comfort, with Jupiter, the planet of power, position, status and luck. He will enjoy a long fulfilling life.

Handprints of Albert Einstein ~ Scientist

Hand impression 1: Hand of Scientist Albert Einstein

Albert Einstein holds a unique position in the world of science. He is regarded as the father of modern science and the most intellectual scientist of all time. The square shape of the hand with a prominent Mount of Upper Mars (energy) and Mount of the Moon (mind), denotes a person of tireless mental energy. Pads or soft bulges on the fingertips, indicate interest in music. It is confirmed by reports that music played an important part in Einstein's life. Who can say whether the natural nutrient for the mind to grow is music? Statistics and studies reveal that music has a great impact on the mind and intellectual growth.

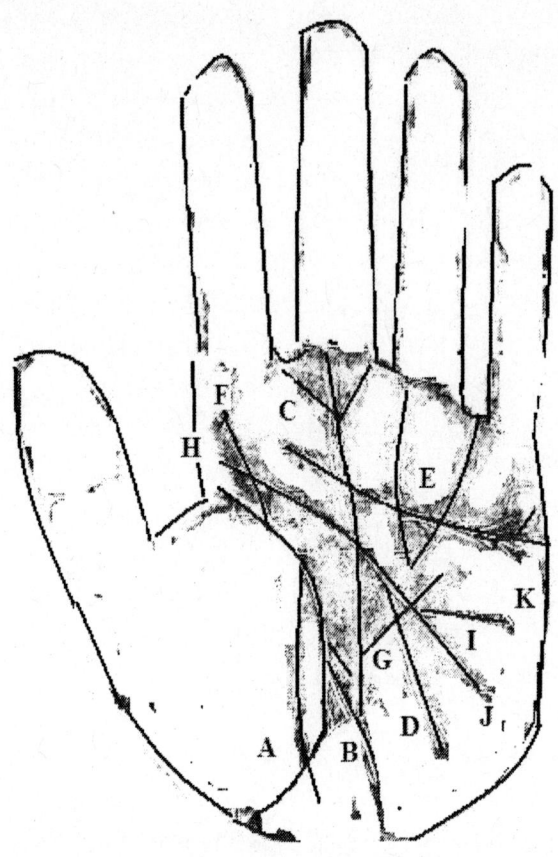

Illustration 9: Lines on the hand of Albert Einstein

For the student of palmistry, Albert Einstein's is the most interesting hand, for he was truly a most gifted soul, born with a purpose (see Illustration 9). He was not only gifted but also lucky, for he was able to fulfill his ambition and purpose. Look at the Life Line first (llustration 9), it has a fish shape (A), which shows a life and destiny away from one's birth place. A branch line from the Line of Life going towards the Mount of the Moon (B), shows leaving his place of birth to pursue his dream. His Fate Line also begins from this Line of Travel. Destiny is marked away from his birth place. Albert Einstein was born in Germany but renounced his German citizenship and moved to Zurich in the early years of his life. Many may be born with intelligence but luck does not always support them. Life opens doors of opportunities only for some, for past *karmas* are carried forward into one's present birth. Einstein's Life Line throws out a branch towards the Mount of Jupiter (Illustration 9 / Line F) – for such a person, social status and a position of power come naturally. After the World War II ended, Albert Einstein became a leading figure in the World Government Movement. He was also offered the Presidency of the State of Israel, which he declined.

The striking feature of this hand is the Line of Head which begins with a gap from the Line of Life, below the Mount of Jupiter (see H). Again, notice the significance of the Mount of Jupiter in this example (like examples 1 and 2 of Obama and Putin). However, there is a difference between a world leader and a world famous scientist. How? His long Line of head slopes and ends in a fork (see Illustration 9/ Line I). This fork is unique and denotes a person of extreme intelligence. Both the left and right hands have similar forked and long Lines of Head. This implies the person is born a genius. One hand suggests the qualities one is born with and the other hand the qualities one develops in the present birth. If both hands have similar qualities, this suggests the person utilizes the qualities that he is born with. In Einstein's hand, one prong of this fork ends on the Upper Mount of Mars – Mars is also the natural ruler of science in occult sciences (see K), and the other prong ends on the Mount of the Moon/mind (see J). This denotes a person of great intelligence.

One of the most amazing and interesting features of his hand is his fate line. Fate line ends in a sign of *trishul* or a trident, see 'C' illustration 9, one of the most rare and sacred sign in Hindu palmistry, gives all three— —name, fame and prosperity- in life and fame even after death. This is one rare marking, I have found, extremely lucky for its possessor.

At point G (see Illustration 9), the Fate Line throws a branch line towards the Mount of Mercury, the mount of scientific research. For success in scientific research (see E), there is the mark of Vishnu (V), again a most sacred sign. This V mark has one prong going towards the mount of scientific research (Mount of Mercury) and the other towards the mount of success and fame (Mount of the Sun). The *trishul* and V mark of Hindu diety, Vishnu, are rare markings and the beautiful fork at the end of the Head Line shows a genius born with a destiny. Albert Einstein gave the world the *Theory of Relativity*, bringing revolution to the field of physics. He was recipient of the Nobel Prize (Physics), for his work in theoretical physics and the discovery of the Law of Photoelectric Effect.

Hand of Sonia Gandhi ~ President, Indian Congress Party

Photo 9: Palm of Sonia Gandhi
Source: *palmistryforyou.com/.../hand-analysis-of-sonia-gandhi.html*

Sonia Gandhi, President of the Indian Congress Party and the Chairperson of the ruling United Progressive Alliance, was named the third most powerful woman in the world by

Forbes magazine in 2004. She was born in a small village in Italy, married Rajiv Gandhi, the son of then Prime Minister of India, Indira Gandhi, and moved to India. Rajiv became Prime Minister himself and was then violently assassinated.

Photo 10: Hand of Sonia Gandhi
Source: http://www.daylife.com/topic/Sonia_Gandhi/photos

The most interesting feature in Sonia Gandhi's hand, for a student of palmistry, is the shape of her hand, the thumb and the Head Line. The hand is square shaped. A branch line from the Line of Life moves towards the Mount of the Moon – such a person makes her destiny away from the land of her birth. This marking is similar to scientist Einstein's, who also lived his life away from his birth place. Sonia Gandhi moved to India after her marriage.

I have discussed two other world leaders – US President Obama and Russian Prime Minister, Vladimir Putin – like them, Sonia Gandhi also possesses a powerful Mount of Jupiter. Like the US President, her Line of Head also begins from the Mount of Jupiter and like both the others, she also has a double Line of Life. Sonia Gandhi also had a humble start.

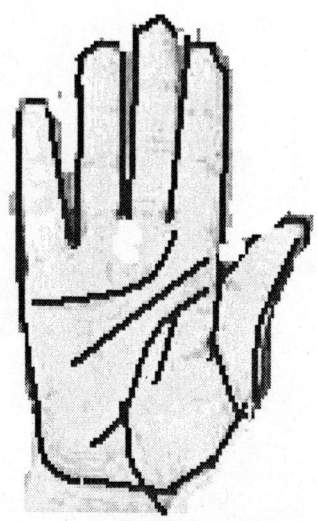

Illustration 10: Hand of Sonia Gandhi

The head line commences with a wide gap, from the Line of Life (see Illustration 10). This line, in combination with the type of hand, gives a clear indication of a strong personality and independence of thought. The thumb and the fourth finger are exceptionally long. As per ancient palmistry texts and also in my professional experience, a person holding position and social status never has a weak thumb. The length of the little finger always strengthens the promise of a powerful government position. The Line of Head starting from the seat of power, the Mount of Jupiter, alone is a strong indication that the person, irrespective of social and economic position at the time of birth, will rise to a position of power and gain social status. Under her leadership, the Congress-led UPA government came to power in 2009, with a near majority in the Indian parliament.

Hand Cast of Michael Jackson ~ Musician

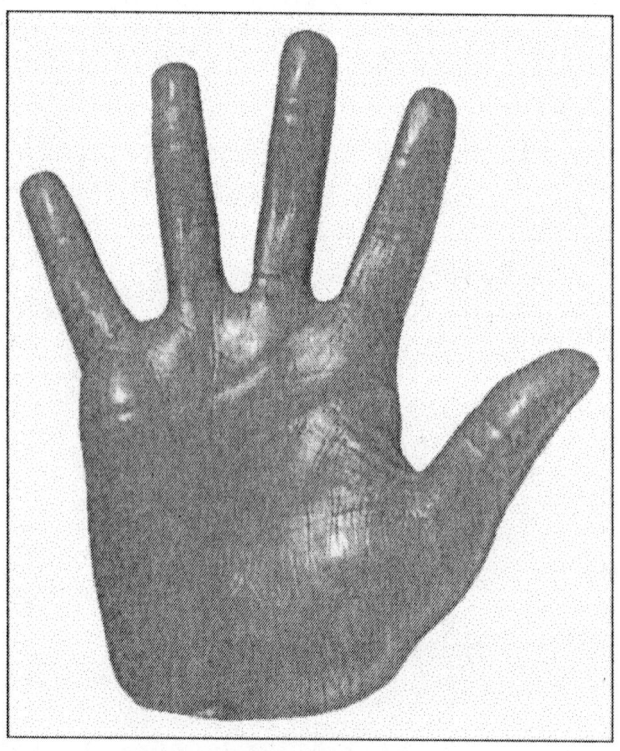

Michael Jackson was one of the most popular singer-artist-dancers in the history of American pop music. He is often referred to as *King of Pop*. Though American, his popularity crossed borders and he was one of the most successful entertainers of all time. The most decided and characteristic feature of Michael Jackson's hand was the double Head Line and Line of the Sun. It is rare and uncommon to possess double Lines of Head. This denotes intelligence and clearly the two Head Lines, in combination with the shape of the hand, show that Michael Jackson was a man of great creative intelligence.

PALMISTRY The Mystery of Destiny

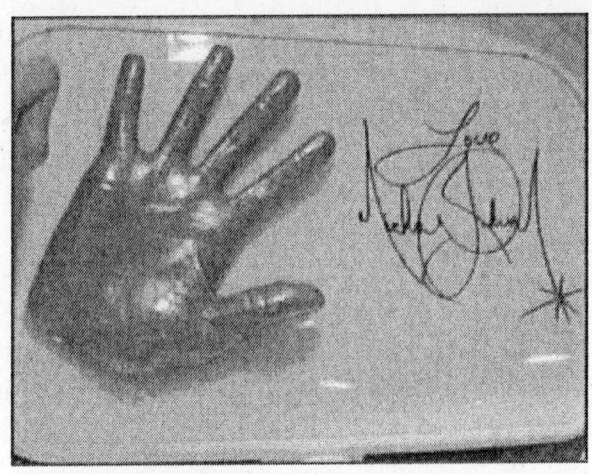

**Photo 10: Michael Jackson's hand cast,
at Madame Tussauds, London**
Source: http://handfacts.wordpress.com/category/hand-reading/page/3/

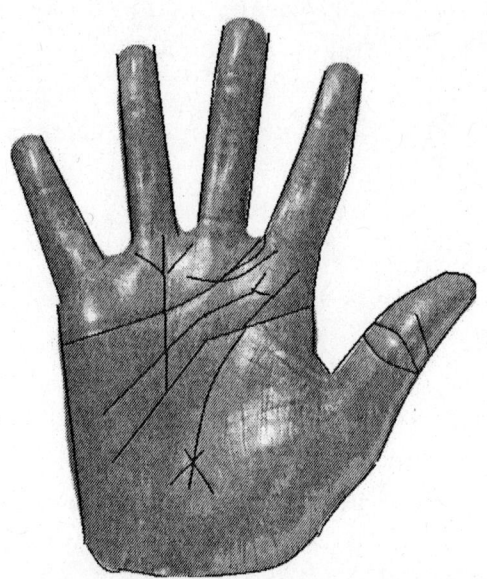

Illustration 10: Michael Jackson's hand cast

One Head Line commences from the Line of Life and the other from the Mount of Jupiter – the mount of power and social status (again, notice the significance of this mount). The Line of Head commencing from the Mount of Jupiter is in the shape of the mouth of a serpent, *Rahu*, which gives position in society but the serpent shape signifies personal worries. The Wheat Line on the thumb has the beautiful shape of a flower and denotes fame and luck in life. But this line has two parallel lines to it and this shows heavy expenditures. When there are two Wheat Lines and these lines do not meet at the end but are parallel to each other, the person acquires immense wealth but his expenditures and the outflow of wealth too, is huge. This famous musician was also a notable humanitarian and philanthropist. The Wheat Line on the thumb is in the shape of an eye – the other line supporting the eye, increases the financial net worth. Parallel lines show both inflow and outflow of money.

The Sun Line of fame and talent, ends in a *trishul* or trident. As I mentioned in example 3, about scientist Albert Einstein – this sign on the Fate or Sun Line signifies name, fame and prosperity – not only in the lifetime of the individual but even after death. Such a person leaves his mark and is remembered by future generations. Such people are born with rare talent and make huge contributions in the creative field they chose. *The trishul* is one of the most sacred signs of Hindu palmistry and in Michael jackson's hand, this marking is on the Sun Line of creativity which indicates fame and creative talent. The sign of the *trishul* or trident, at the end of Sun Line, is rare and is a most interesting palmistry sign which denotes unprecedented talent and fame.

A clear branch line from the Line of Life reaches the Mount of Jupiter, ensuring great social status. Like all earlier examples, this example too shows the significance of the Mount of Jupiter.

An island and a bar on the Line of Heart are ominous and unfavorable signs affecting longevity. I have discussed this in detail in chapters 4 and 10. In palmistry, the sign of a star on the Line of Life indicates sudden and untimely death. On Michael Jackson's Line of Life, the sign of a star and a bar on the Heart Line (heart failure) (see Illustration 10), tells of untimely death. However, the sign of the *trishul* at the end of the line of the Sun makes him immortal in the hearts of millions of his fans.

Hand of Charles, Prince Of Wales

Photo 11: Charles, the Prince of Wales
Source: http://www.google.co.in

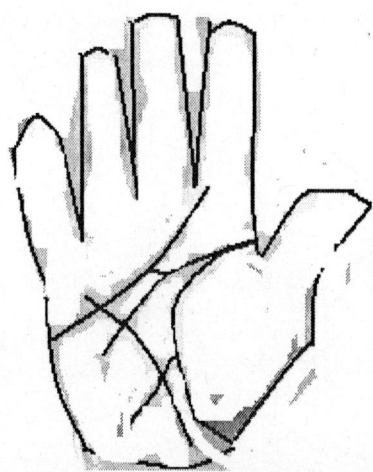

Illustration 11: Hand of Prince Charles

The hand of Prince Charles is of special interest to those studying palmistry. The first noticeable features of his hand are the mounts and the shape. The shape of the hand suggests a fondness for outdoor sports and activities. He has a broad, heavy and well-padded hand. He is reported to enjoy hunting, shooting, fishing, polo and skiing. It is the hand of a painter or artist. The shape of the thumb is like a sword. This denotes a balanced, pliable nature and adaptability to others. He is not obstinate in his views. A person with such a thumb is born with a clear destiny in life and he accepts the challenges of life and has a temperament adaptable to others (see Photo 11).

All the mounts of the hand are very well-developed and indicate easily acquired wealth. The Mount of Jupiter signifies social position, status and power. The Mount of Saturn, when it is well developed as it is here, means immense wealth. The Mount of Mercury gives eloquence. Imagination from the Mount of the Moon is very well balanced by the love of outdoor and physical sports in the very well developed Mounts of Upper and Lower Mars. In being born in a palace, a soul brings good *karma* from his past births.

Why are some born in palace with riches and others in poverty? What is it that decides the destiny of a soul? It is *karma*. Our present actions may subtract or add to past *karma* regarding our birth, but it is past *karma* that seals our fate as to who are our parents. The destiny of the soul also has two parts – one that is in our hand and the other that cannot be changed. After all, who would ask for losses, diseases or sorrow in life? But still it happens – are we able to change that? No, but probably we can try, through our present *karma*, to fare well when adversity strikes.

Charles is the eldest son of Queen Elizabeth II and is known as the Prince of Wales. He was born into riches and wealth plus social status. His Line of Head starts close to the Line of Life and remains connected for a great distance. Even the Line of Fate/destiny, follows its path close to the Line of Life – this indicates the influence of family in early life (see Photo 11 & Ilustration 11). Family has a greater influence in important matters regarding such a person. This I have discussed in detail in Part I. The Line of Head on Prince Charles' hand may interest readers. My earlier examples in this section show how the Line of Head is significant in marking destiny, even with the most humble beginnings. In Charles' hand, he is born into affluence and riches (all mounts strong) and the voice of his royal family in the major decisions of his life is indicated by the unusually long and connected Head Line Line of life.

The Line of Head is long but curved towards the Line of Heart. This indicates high intellect and emotions influencing the decisions in life. The Lines of Head and Heart, are connected by a small line – this brings extreme sorrow and disappointments in matters of the heart. Charles married Lady Diana Spencer in a fairy-tale wedding, but this marriage came to an end. A year later, Lady Diana died in a car crash. Charles is now married to his long-time love, Camilla Parker-Bowles.

The Line of Fate forms the shape of a fish tail with a branch from Line of Life. The sign of a fish in Hindu palmistry is considered a very lucky sign, denoting riches. The direction of the Fate Line is towards the Mount of Mercury – this is rare and shows the person has immense wealth and riches. The sign of a fish and the Fate Line running towards the Mount of Mercury, are considered extremely lucky signs in terms of wealth. The royal status is seen on Charles' palm in the well padded and well developed mounts – especially the Mount of Jupiter.

Hand of Hollywood Actress ~ Nicole Kidman

12: Photo of hollywood actress, Nicole Kidman Source:http:/
/www.google.co.in/imgres?imgurl=http://4.bp.blogspot.com Photo

The hand of Hollywood actress is an interesting study. First thing to notice is the colour of the hand (not seen here in black and white) – the hand is extremely red. Such a person is full of energy and temperamental in nature. The red colour of the hand denotes a restless nature, and this also gives originality of ideas and confidence to succeed. Nicole Kidman appeared in several Australian productions along with her success in the Hollywood film industry. She is also the face of many beauty products which she endorses. She has won many awards and critical praise for her portrayals in the course of her career.

The shape of the hand is artistic or conic with long pointed fingers. Such a person pays attention to even the most minute detail and finds creative satisfaction in this. The long and beautifully pointed fingers indicate great creative talent. Nicole Kidman's long pointed fingers and the red colour of her palm, indicate her passion for her work and also a love of adventure and risk-taking. Nicole Kidman mentioned in an interview on a television show with Ellen DeGeneres, that while shooting for a movie, she is banned from indulging in one of her favorite hobbies – sky diving. Such a person should always be careful of wounds and injuries.

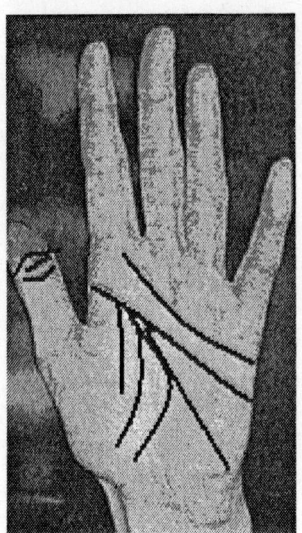

Illustration 12: Hand of Nicole Kidman

The Line of Head (see Illustration 12), is very, very long and slopes gently. The Wheat Line on the thumb has the shape of an eye, with a supporting line in-between – according to Hindu palmistry, this is one of the most auspicious lines for professional success. Destiny holds the hands of such a person. The Line of Head sloping towards the Mount of the Moon (imagination), denotes success in the field of acting.

A line from the Life Line runs towards the Mount of the Moon, quite early in life. This line indicates travel from an early age. Nicole Kidman was born in the USA. At the time of her birth, her father was a Visiting Fellow in the United States. The family returned to Australia when Kidman was four. As a result of being born to Australian parents in the USA, the actress holds dual citizenship of Australia and the United States.

In her hand (see Illustration11 & Photo 11), there are two lines dropping from the Line of Life towards the Mount of Venus. These are lines of marriage and are experienced passionately by her (remember the colour of the hand). The actress was married twice. Her earlier marriage to Hollywood actor, Tom Cruise, lasted 11 years, and her current marriage is to country musician, Keith Urban, with whom she has a daughter. The length of the second line of affection on the Mount of Venus is favourable.

Hand of former Prime Minister of Pakistan ~ Benazir Bhutto

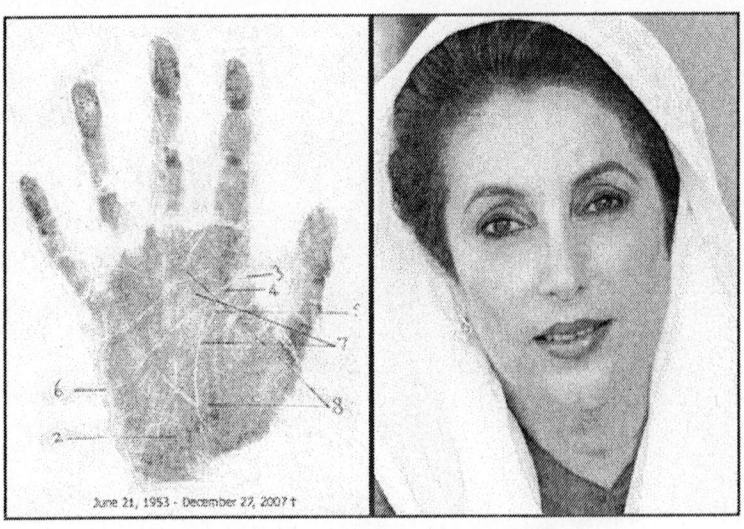

Photo 13: Benazir Bhutto
Source : http://www.handresearch.com/news/benazir-bhutto-palmprint-of-destiny.htm

Benazir Bhutto was a Pakistani politician. She was twice elected Prime Minister of Pakistan. The most noticeable feature of her hand is the thumb (see Photo14). Benazir Bhutto had a very long thumb covering almost three-fourth the length of the first finger. She was the first woman elected to head a Muslim state, and to date, the first and only woman Prime Minister of Pakistan. The first and the third fingers (see Photo 14), lean towards the middle finger. The third finger stands slightly away with a gap. This shows political motivation and independence of thought and action. She has a long Line of Head starting below the mount of power –

the Mount of Jupiter (see Illustration 13). One should notice, as in earlier examples of hands of world leaders, the importance of the long thumb and long Head Line, starting from below the Mount of Jupiter, in placing the person in a position of power.

Photo 14: The shape of the hand is more noticeable here

Benazir was assassinated before a scheduled Pakistani general election, in which she was a leading opposition candidate. Longevity can be predicted from the thumb, the Line of Heart and the Line of Life. The *Malika Rekha* has an

PALMISTRY The Mystery of Destiny

island cut by lines coming from the Mount of Mars (see Illustration 13 A [ref. Chapter 2 / *Lines on the Thumb in Hindu Palmistry*]). This suggests a violent death. Lines from the Lower Mount of Mars gives the indication of a violent death – reconfirmed by the much rayed Mount of Saturn below the second finger, and the Line of Heart cut short by bars (C). As already dealt with, the point where the Line of Health cuts the Line of Life, indicates age at the time of death.

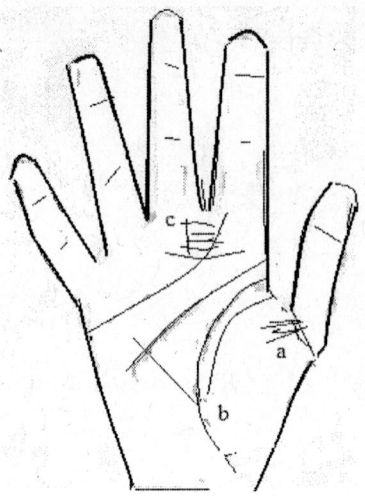

Illustration 13: Hand of Benazir Bhutto

The double Line of Life or supporting line to the Life Line, as in earlier examples, gave her a position of power and security, but at the age when this line ends at B, the Line of Health meets the Line of Life – this is a sign of death. The Lines of Heart, Head and Life, all confirm life cut short through violence. Benazir Bhutto was assassinated while leaving a campaign rally, cutting short her life in a violent manner.

Hand of Hillary Clinton ~
Secretary of State and former First Lady, United States of America

Photo 14: Hand of Hillary Clinton
Source: http://www.handresearch.com/news/Menu_bestanden/hillary-clinton-left-hand.jpg

Hillary Clinton is presently serving as the Secretary of State in the administration of President Barrack Obama. She was a United States Senator for New York and a leading candidate for the Democratic presidential nomination in the 2008 elections. As wife of the former President, Bill Clinton, she has been First Lady as well.

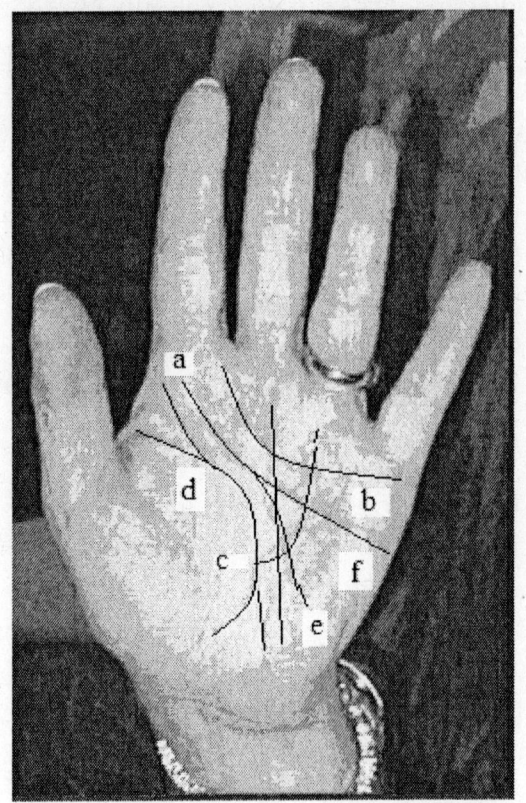

Illustration 14: Hand of Hillary Clinton

The hand of Hillary Clinton is an interesting study (see Illustration 14). Notice the long thumb and Head Line starting from the Mount of power – Jupiter (A). The thumb has a broad and bulging face – such a person becomes a leader or guide to others. The long Head Line divides into two parts – one prong runs towards the Mount of Mars and the other prong runs towards the Mount of the Moon. This indicates great intellectual courage balanced by her imaginative faculties in pursuit of her goals.

A fine Line of Heart begins near the Line of Marriage (B) – in palmistry this indicates marriage to a man who earns name and position. The slight curve of the Heart Line towards the powerful Head Line, indicates that whenever there is a fight between heart and mind, the mind wins. Emotional matters will not interfere in the pursuit of her goals. The state of her marriage was the subject of considerable speculation following the Lewinsky scandal. This curve of line indicates emotional stress and the Heart Line curving close to the Line of Head indicates the mind ruling over matters of the heart.

At point D, a branch from the Life Line runs towards the Mount of Jupiter – such a person fulfills her ambitions. At point C, a line from the Life Line branches towards the Mount of the Sun. This refers to the age when, through her own efforts, she herself attains name and position in the world. Hillary Clinton was the first woman to be elected to represent the state of New York. This election also marked the first time an American First Lady had run for public office. She then became the first former First Lady to serve in the cabinet of the President.